High
and Wild

"That new vision of the world
won through hardship . . ."

Antoine de Saint-Exupéry

High and Wild

ESSAYS ON WILDERNESS ADVENTURE

GALEN ROWELL

With an Introduction by Robert Redford

LEXIKOS
San Francisco

Second edition, revised and expanded

Published in 1983 by
Lexikos
703 Market Street
San Francisco, California 94103

Cover design by Laurie Anderson. Text design by Alan
Magary. Text set in Baskerville with Helvetica by Miller
Freeman Composition. Printed on 60-pound Sterling Litho
Matte by Edward Brothers, Inc.

Cover illustration: Bristlecone pine at sunrise, White
Mountains, California; photo by Galen Rowell. *Frontispiece:*
Split rock and cirrus cloud, Owens Valley, California; photo
by Galen Rowell.

Portions of this book have appeared in altered form in
Sierra and *Sierra Club Bulletin, Quest, Ascent, Backpacker,
Mariah, Mountain Gazette,* and *American Alpine Journal.*

Manufactured in the United States of America.

Library of Congress Cataloging in Publication Data

    High and wild.
    Rev. ed. of: High and wild : a mountaineer's world.
c1979.
    1. Mountaineering—United States. 2. Mountaineering
—Canada. 3. Mountaineering—Asia. 4. Mountains—
United States—Recreational use. 5. Mountains—
Canada—Recreational use. 6. Mountains—Asia—
Recreational use. I. Title

GV191.4.R68 1983 796.5′22′097 83-80855
ISBN 0-938530-21-6

83 84 85 86 87 5 4 3 2 1

for Nicole and Tony

Contents

Introduction

THERE IS A symbiotic relationship between nature and art. Every now and then someone will emerge who embodies this alliance. Galen Rowell is one such. Photographer, essayist, naturalist, opportunist. He is all of these. But more. In his life, his work, his spirit, he suggests something new—a composite. That rare breed that combines these qualities to bring us a new light—a gift.

In the Fall of 1982, I had the pleasure of meeting Galen Rowell—a willing guide to the high Khumbu region of Nepal, in the intense solitary atmosphere of a culture old and a space remote from the complications of a mechanized society. On a late afternoon somewhere around 15,000 feet I had the privilege of witnessing something awesome. We stopped, an extra sense signalling that high above us on a steep hillside was a mountain tahr, scarce and elusive. Rowell sensed his presence. I had no clue. He loaded his camera with blurring intensity, never taking his eyes off the animal that I still had trouble finding. Then Rowell was gone—off the trail and up the cliff— quickly. And quietly. I watched as he stalked the reluc-

Robert Redford at 18,500 feet in the Khumbu region, Nepal. Mt. Everest in is background.

tant animal, moving with great speed and agility at an altitude that doesn't allow for it. He seemed to contradict gravity and physical law. He would wait and watch and move and disappear and reappear—always closer. The animal was grazing and standing still. Finally I saw that the man and the animal were practically face to face—a great sensitivity prevailed as Galen shot picture after picture, always watching and the animal calmly watching in return. The pictures were taken. Rare. Beautiful. How did it happen? I sensed respect and understanding and felt a positive joy to be able to be there to see it.

In this new edition of *High and Wild*, the most personal of his books, Rowell gives us an opening to that amazing grace—the ability to move through nature and capture moments seldom seen. He takes us beyond, to a rarified place that our own eye cannot spot—and does so without disturbing what is there.

I feel his work is about to happen—the appreciation now to expand. I am grateful for his talent, his mind, and his sensitivity. And for that which he shares with us.

Robert Redford

Sundance, Utah
July 1983

Preface

THIS IS NOT a guide-book. There are plenty of those to tell you what to bring, where to go, and how to get there. The high and wild places of this book are a different kind of wilderness. Wilderness is more than a physical place; it is a state of mind. In fact, it is the original state of mind—the one in which we evolved.

My intent was not only to record images and descriptions of little-known places or adventures. I wanted to provide a different perspective, a more immediate and intuitive view of the activities that form the basis of wilderness exploration: mountain climbing, backpacing, skiing. And thinking.

We have come to think of climbing and skiing as highly competitive. But these activities are far more basic than that: they began as simple methods to reach places otherwise inaccessible. The skills themselves are only tools; they connect us to the world of wilderness. The most sophisticated equipment is only an aid to, not a substitute for, our physical and mental resources. The ability to adapt to things as they are—a practical necessity in wilderness exploration—also

Galen Rowell rockclimbing on the east side of the Sierra Nevada, California.

teaches us how to live more perceptively. In high and wild places, adventure is life itself.

To this paperback edition I have added four essays on Himalayan adventures and a glossary of mountaineering terms. The "Note on Photography" in the back matter is slightly revised from the 1979 hardcover edition. My techniques have not changed, although for this edition the color originals, many of which are new, are reproduced in black-and-white conversions to the printer's best ability.

Galen Rowell

Berkeley, California

High
and Wild

"I became less and less concerned with the
mastery of technical difficulty,
or even the ascent of individual peaks,
but more and more absorbed in the
problems and delights of movement
over wide areas of mountain country."

Eric Shipton
That Untravelled World

1
The
New Age
of Mountain
Exploration

NINE MEN gazed at an endless panorama of snowy mountains glowing in the evening sun. Giant glaciers dropped from the flanks of the peaks, covering hundreds of square miles with ice. Except for the men and their equipment, the entire tableau could have been transported from the ice ages of the Pleistocene. The scene's splendor was much more than mere prettiness; it reflected the free expression of natural forces—forces at odds with the men standing for the first time on the summit of Canada's highest mountain, Mount Logan.

A storm was brewing. Black sky oozed toward the men, and they dared not linger at the top, an elevation of nearly 20,000 feet. Mount Logan is more like a range than a single mountain; an eleven-mile section lies above 16,000 feet. The storm overtook the party as it descended in the subarctic twilight, forcing a bivouac in the open at 19,000 feet. The next day they reached their high camp, only to find it torn apart by the blizzard. Another night was spent in the open. When the frostbitten men finally reached their base camp, they found it, too, ravaged by the storm.

Opposite page: Moon, mountain, and shadow, Cirque of the Unclimbables, Northwest Territories, Canada.

At this point, a modern expedition would have radioed a bush pilot, flown out to civilization, and received hospital treatment for frostbite. Even without a radio, the expedition would have faced nothing worse than a boring, painful wait for an aircraft to arrive at a prearranged time. For the nine men of Albert MacCarthy's successful expedition, however, the ordeal was far from over.

The year was 1925, and they were one hundred fifty miles from civilization: only a handful of humans had ever seen Mount Logan from closer than fifty miles. In summer the approach to the mountain had been far too rough for pack animals, so MacCarthy and his companions waited until winter snows had carpeted the rugged canyon floors and glacial moraines, and then spent seventy winter days laying in caches over one hundred thirty miles of the route. In temperatures that often dipped to −40° F, he and three others slowly worked their way toward the mountain, first using horses, then dog teams when the going got rougher.

Only Greenland and Antarctica are more heavily iced than the thousands of square miles of glaciated highlands surrounding Mount Logan, and both the approach and retreat were like a polar expedition. After forty-four days of ice and snow, MacCarthy's weary party finally touched earth again in June, but the ordeal continued. The expedition decided to speed its retreat by floating the rapids of the Chitina River. Makeshift rafts were built with frostbitten hands, but soon one overturned with men, food, equipment, and cameras aboard. The men swam to safety and completed the long journey to McCarthy, Alaska, on foot.

For the last decade, a high-altitude scientific research camp, supplied by helicopter, has operated each summer at 17,600 feet on Mount Logan. The advent of air travel and modern communication systems have made remoteness increasingly difficult to attain. Remoteness, after all, is more than mere physical distance; it is also a function of psychological and technological separation from the rest of humanity.

In time, in isolation, in everything but measured distance, the Logan climbers were more remote than astronauts on the moon.

We are now witnessing the slow death of exploration on earth, and with it the ethos that powered the early polar expeditions and the Mount Logan pioneers. Exploration on foot has become a nostalgic anachronism. Most scientific endeavors associated with it—mapping, surveying, prospecting, photographing, biological research—have welcomed mechanization with open arms. Contemporary climbers use modern transportation and communication to reach the mountains, but they generally agree that the climbing itself must be kept free from motorized or highly technological equipment.

The experience of the first Mount Logan climbers can never be duplicated. Too much of the mountain and its surroundings are too familiar to too many people. But regardless of civilization's encroachment on even the wildest mountain areas, mountaineering has remained essentially a wilderness activity, and its natural setting is all-important. If this were not the case, climbing would be merely an athletic event, as satisfying on tall buildings or inside gymnasiums as on mountains.

It is no accident that many key people in the environmental movement have strong backgrounds in mountaineering, where the very essence of the experience depends on the natural character of the terrain. John Muir, David Brower, Dick Leonard, and Ansel Adams are just a few of the prominent conservationists who climbed mountains extensively, making tangible contacts with the current of evolution and deriving self-knowledge from personal interaction with the harsh, tilted world of rock, snow, ice, and sky. The birth and early years of the Sierra Club took place in this mountain crucible.

For many years, I assumed there must be a direct connection between western culture and climbing. Conditioned by American public education, I contented myself with suppositions as arrogant as any entertained by pre-Victorian biologists. I placed great importance on the notion that mountaineering achievements paralleled the growth of industrialized and urban societies. I assumed that climbing was a triumph of rationality over primitive superstition and was the epitome of a goal-oriented society in which events and discoveries had a cumulative value. After all, I had been taught that mankind mastered the world by passing information from generation to generation, enabling modern western man, the latest beneficiary of this process, to understand the basic principles of nature. Armed with such notions, I concluded that only men in this highly evolved and obviously superior state would knowingly expose their mortal bodies to the terrifying forces of nature. I saw climbing as an expression of modern man's understanding of these forces.

I noted that dogs who follow their masters in the mountains seem to have an instinctive sense of where to stop. They might climb one small cliff, but balk completely at one only slightly higher. I attributed this innate prudence to all living things and reasoned that natural selection might favor it. (If this were true, the best climbers would be those with perfectly ordered, logical minds. The opposite is closer to the truth.)

Several events made me re-examine my assumptions about climbers—both animal and human. One occurred in Alaska as a bush pilot flew me to a remote mountain. We flew past the last spruce trees, beyond the final green splotches of alpine vegetation into an arctic world. Wolverine tracks began in the snow and continued for miles to the head of a large glacier, far beyond any source of food. Like our own advance into a hostile environment the tracks seemed unexplainable. I thought I had witnessed an isolated event, but later I talked to a climber who had seen a single wolf at 10,000 feet on Mount McKinley. Searching for a motive but finding none, I supposed the wolf and the wolverine had merely been lost.

Opposite page:
Mountain goat
climbing a 5.8
crack.

Then I spent a day watching a mountain goat in a wild range of mountains in the Canadian North, and for once I felt I had a clear understanding of nature's

logic. Goats climb to avoid predators and to feed on the lush alpine vegetation. I was not at all surprised when my actions in a meadow frightened a goat onto a steep cliff. I watched him run across a headwall on which my companions and I had used ropes and pitons only a few days earlier. With almost sadistic pleasure I approached the bottom of the cliff and guarded the only possible descent from the bulging, 2000-foot rock face. The goat tried every conceivable way of climbing down, but instead of stopping at a point where he began to feel uneasy, he pushed himself, as a climber would, trying something one grade above his standard. I nervously watched him pivot on a hopelessly narrow stance and attempt a traverse that eventually ended in flawless granite. While wandering around the base, I made a discovery: the broken, mummified body of another goat that evidently had fallen from the same cliff. After several hours of watching, I returned to camp, still in sight of the goat, but half a mile away.

Instead of immediately descending and continuing in the direction he was originally headed, the goat stayed on the wall for quite some time. When he did come down, he looked to see if we were still watching. We were too far away to offer any threat to his passage, but he followed the base of the cliff in the direction opposite to where he was originally headed. At the first crack system he began to climb again, this time a flashy, three-hundred-foot romp. At the top of a pedestal he pivoted a full circle, like a fashion model, then bounded down the cliff again. He repeated his climbing antics in other spots, seeming always to make sure that we were watching. Finally, he ambled off in the direction he had originally taken. Where was the instinctive animal prudence I had posited?

The goat's antics appeared to have no survival value. If anything, I thought they were the dangerous frolics of an alpine show-off, but on further reflection I realized my response to the goat's climbing was similar to the public's reaction to human mountaineering. Products of the technological age, we are always ready to condemn as frivolous any activity whose purpose cannot be explained with reason and logic. I knew why I climbed, even if I couldn't express it in words. But as a prisoner of the modern, I believed that the urge had to be logically explainable. "Because it is there!" is a useless platitude. An answer closer to the truth came from a glider pilot who was asked by a television interviewer why he liked to do loops fifty feet above the ground; he simply answered, "I guess I'm just an adrenalin freak!"

Mountaineering may be the final step in terrestrial exploration, but it is increasingly becoming an end in itself. It is futile to explain climbing as either the triumph of rationality over superstition or the triumph of primitiveness over an increasingly artificial world. It is at once neither and both. It is Mac-Carthy's party on Mount Logan in 1925; crag climbers in New York in 1979; de Saussure making scientific observations on Mont Blanc in 1787; sourdoughs climbing Mount McKinley's north peak in 1910; Whymper, who longed to be a polar explorer, climbing the Matterhorn in 1865; Whillans, a Manchester plumber, on Mount Everest in 1972; two children scrambling in a national park campground; Toni Egger disappearing on Cerro Torre in icy Patagonia; an

Yosemite Valley after an early fall snowstorm.

Indian hunting party on top of Mount Whitney; a solo climber on Yosemite's El Capitan.

The common thread of these diverse experiences is human interaction with mountains. But not all such interaction is considered mountaineering. The north wall of the Eiger is one of the most famous climbs in Europe, but those who traverse it via the railway tunnel that pierces its face can hardly be called mountaineers. Climbers adapt their behavior to wild surroundings rather than changing the face of the land to ease their passage. Most questions of climbing ethics and style revolve around this concept. Techniques that alter the environment—even temporarily—are not considered as good style as those that leave no sign of passage. Examples of environment-altering techniques are step-cutting in ice; expansion bolts, which require holes drilled into rock; expeditionary climbing, which depends on establishing temporary tent cities at strategic locations and moving a pyramid of men and supplies upward until the summit is within easy striking distance; and the use of fixed ropes, which enable climbers to ascend the rope instead of the rock or snow.

Unlike skiing, kayaking, and many other outdoor sports, climbing is not fundamentally dependent on equipment. A skier can't ski without skis, but a climber can climb without ropes or pitons. Much climbing is done without any special equipment at all. At least half of the five hundred "technical" climbs in Yosemite Valley could be climbed solo, unroped and barefoot, by a highly skilled climber, although this would be as risky as a circus acrobat performing without a net. The next step beyond climbing without equipment is to carry it only for safety—as an acrobat uses his net for security—rather than for direct climbing aid. This is often the most satisfying kind of climbing: raw adventure achieved with a few classic tools. Simplicity is the hallmark of good climbing equipment. A nylon climbing rope is a simple tool that does a complex job. It is a flexible, portable, energy-absorbing device capable of diffusing sudden shock loads of thousands of pounds. Similarly, an ice axe serves as a step-cutting tool, a walking stick, a handhold for technical ice-climbing, and a braking mechanism for a climber falling on snow. By shifting the emphasis from working with the natural scene to tinkering with gear, equipment fetishists alter the basic character of the mountaineering experience.

Collecting an excess of fancy new equipment, however pointless in itself, is only one symptom of a more serious ailment. Perhaps because they can no longer look forward to the rewards of explorers, modern climbers feel compelled to measure themselves in other ways—usually not so much by skill and dedication as by lists of conquests. Climbs are numbered, measured, and categorized; and for many, the goal becomes all-important, the game only secondary. What Aleister Crowley, the eccentric Englishman, stated early in the century holds true today: "Climbing itself is being very much spoilt by the attitude of the [British] Alpine Club in insisting that the achievement, not the enjoyment, is the important thing. This is the American Spirit, to count and compare instead of being content with spiritual satisfaction."

Crowley may have overstated his case, for spiritual satisfaction is a synergism involving both self-experience and achievement. And competition is often a necessary catalyst for the biggest climbs, providing motivation for an activity that is useless in practical terms. But he is right that the self-knowledge derived from personal interaction with natural forces is a more important component of alpinism than is competition with the rated and timed achievements of others.

The renowned British climber A.F. Mummery, who climbed in the Alps a century ago, once wrote:

> The true Mountaineer is the man who attempts new ascents. Equally, whether he succeeds or fails, he delights in the fun and jollity of the struggle. The gaunt, bare slabs, the square, precipitous steps in the ridge, and the black, bulging ice of the gully, are the very breath of life to his being. I do not pretend to be able to analyze this

Mule deer bucks at 12,000 feet in the Palisade Range, High Sierra.

feeling, still less to be able to make it clear to unbelievers. It must be felt to be understood, but it is potent to happiness and sends the blood tingling through the veins, destroying every trace of cynicism and striking at the very roots of pessimistic philosophy.

Mummery sounds a theme that is becoming increasingly popular today: The true mountaineer, whether he succeeds or fails, delights in the struggle. Of course there is some extra elation in a hard-won achievement, but the emphasis is more on the effort itself than on its ends. The first ascent of a mountain is only the beginning. Almost endless variations are possible: new routes, solo climbs, winter climbs, all-free ascents, pitonless ascents, alpine-style climbs of mountains previously climbed by expeditionary sieges. Many of the adventures described in this book represent "new twists" to old challenges and are all the more rewarding for being so.

Many young climbers feel unlucky not to have been part of the so-called Golden Age, roughly from 1860 to 1960, when most of the world's important mountains and rock walls were climbed for the first time. These particular achievements can never be repeated, but a mountain or cliff is never conquered, though one party of climbers or many manage to sneak through its defenses. Crowley's "spiritual satisfaction" and Mummery's "delight in the struggle" are still available for the modern generation, for the 2000th person on top of Mount McKinley as well as for the first, and for the unnumbered person who solves a boulder problem in a city park.

Every present-day mountaineer is a frustrated explorer at heart, secretly envying the struggles of the Mount Logan climbers and other pioneers of the high wilderness. He intuitively comprehends the mysterious attraction of alpine sanctuaries for the wolverine, the wolf, and the mountain goat. Also intuitively, he plays the climbing games of style without ever having been taught the rules. If he were told he must play the games according to a fixed set of rules, he would surely rebel. He values first ascents, but is more often found doing "old classics" for the sheer joy of climbing. His experiences, not medallions, are his achievements. When he does throw his heart and soul into an especially difficult climb, he feels not only joy, but also regret when it is over. Like Mummery, he delights in the struggle, and many lowland hours are spent in contemplation of his next objective.

The remoteness of Mount Logan in 1925 is gone forever, but a glimpse through the window of the past is still possible. A glint is returning to some climbers' eyes as they go after famed Himalayan mountains in self-contained, alpine-style groups. The trend of not using hammers in rockclimbing leaves many newer routes with no signs of human passage; every person who repeats these climbs can discover them anew, as did the first ascent party. The limiting factor in mountaineering is not first ascents but wilderness, and prime experiences will always be dependent on the preservation of the environment.

This book depicts and celebrates only a few of the world's high and wild places—those I have been privileged to visit. The events reported here are only episodes in the developing drama of mountaineering. As long as wild places remain unchanged by the hand of man, adventurers will continue to experience them in ever-changing ways.

2
Alone
on Bear
Creek Spire

ON A FRIDAY evening in 1971 I drove two hundred miles east from Berkeley, California, on a road as familiar to me as my home street. It led to Yosemite Valley, where I had been climbing on weekends for a decade. As the winding road enters the national park, it parallels the Merced River through a deep gorge, and the canyon broadens into a flat valley surrounded by cliffs that rise to the stars.

Even to those who have been there hundreds of times, the first glimpse of Yosemite is overwhelming. As a child I imagined that the valley at night looked like a movie set. Moonlight reflected from the massive granite forms made them appear too stark and simple to be big; the valley seemed like a small model of itself. I felt I could almost reach out and touch the tops of cliffs 3000 feet overhead.

I stopped at Yosemite Lodge, where I met a group of climbers who gathered there every weekend. Within minutes I was invited to join friends on a route I had done many times before. Though I had intended to climb in Yosemite, I felt a sudden urge to

Opposite page:
South face of
Bear Creek Spire
from the air.

15

Rockclimbing on Yosemite's "Lunatic Fringe."

change that plan and suggested an alternative—the south face of Bear Creek Spire in the John Muir Wilderness adjoining Yosemite National Park. No interest. I might as well have suggested Patagonia.

I sat and thought for a while about why I had lost enthusiasm for a Yosemite climb, and soon realized that I felt a need to escape the security Yosemite represented. It was home—familiar walls, faces, sounds, smells—and I was already part of an earlier generation, from a time when climbers knew the wonder of gazing at great cliffs still untouched by the hand of man. When I first climbed in Yosemite in 1957, none of the big walls had been ascended. Since that time, all of Yosemite's major cliffs had been climbed by at least one route; El Capitan now had eleven; the front face of Half Dome, four. The simply joys of exploration were on the wane; in their place was a trend to count and compare experiences with those of others who had climbed the same routes. I had no doubt that many Yosemite climbs demanded greater skill than the hardest routes of the highest ranges, but a big red flag went up when I saw climbers far more talented than myself unwilling to test in the nearby wilderness the skills acquired in this fair-weather womb. There was little I could do personally to reverse what I considered an unfortunate trend, except to bow out of it. I decided to go to Bear Creek Spire, alone. The decision to solo did not come from any high motive; quite simply, no one would go with me.

I slept fitfully in a crowded campground before driving at dawn toward Tioga Pass, on the park's eastern boundary. The pass, at almost 10,000 feet, was just below timberline; and though summer was nearly over, the meadows were still lush. My climb would begin in just this sort of terrain, but farther south, where not a single road crossed the rugged Sierra crest for two hundred miles. To reach my starting point I drove another hundred miles, first dropping thousands of feet to the desert floor of the Mono Basin, then along the base of the mountains until a dead-end side road brought me back up to 10,400 feet.

Here I locked my ten-speed bicycle to a tree in the woods not far from the roadhead. My plan was to drive on to another trailhead farther south, walk eight miles in and 5000 feet up to the base of Bear Creek Spire, climb it, traverse the north side to pick up my bicycle, and ride forty miles back to my car.

From where I cached my bike, I could see Bear Creek Spire about ten miles away, and before turning around to continue south, I took a long look at it. I had once wondered why this undistinguished 13,713-foot peak, which had been climbed from the west by a moderate scramble in 1923, was named a spire. The answer was clear when I first saw its south face from the ridge of another mountain. The face is a pointed blade of granite, which to the best of my knowledge had never been attempted.

I drove on into America's deepest valley, the Owens Valley, created by a massive fault block between the 14,000-foot summits of the High Sierra and the White Mountains twenty miles to the east. An earthquake greater than the one that almost destroyed San Francisco in 1906 dropped the valley

twenty feet in 1872. I took a side road up Pine Creek
to the largest tungsten mine in North America. Out-
wardly it look like a normal mining operation in a
mountain valley; actually, it is upside-down. Shafts
climb from the tunnels up into the mountains, and
one penetrates Bear Creek Spire, four air miles away.
I left my car and began hiking away from the
creaks and whines of the milling operation. I soon
came upon what looked like a natural marble quarry:
glacial polish had combined with frost-heaving to seg-
ment white aplite into piles of burnished blocks that
gleamed against the surrounding granite. By noon I
left the last whitebark pines below and set out across a
barren moraine composed of loose granite boulders.
When I saw the vivid green of a tiny lake set amid the
glacial debris, I knew that ice somewhere beneath the
surface was still carving the landscape. Glacially
scoured rock dust—"glacier milk"—accounted for
the water's tint.

My memory of how impressive the sough face appeared from a distance had been tempered somewhat
by a recent look at the contour map, which showed
the wall to be about eight hundred feet high and not
particularly steep. Now, at close range, my original
impression returned; the face was fully 1200 feet
high, without a single large ledge. The situation gave
me pause. It was two o'clock in the afternoon, and I
was carrying only minimal equipment: a three-eighth-
inch rope, one quart of water, some food, a short, half
sleeping bag, and a handful of pitons and carabiners. I
foresaw a demanding afternoon on the face under a
hot sun, but nothing to make me seriously consider
giving up the ascent.

The climbing began with deceptive ease. I didn't
even rope up for several hundred feet, because cracks
and handholds kept appearing in just the right places.
A squeeze chimney at nearly 13,000 feet left me pant-
ing, however; and I used rope and pitons for safety on
the steep face above. I made steady progress until I
reached a small pedestal and discovered a smooth
headwall above; I tried to free-climb it with the rope
for safety, but failed. The only crack I could spot was

separated from better terrain above by about eight feet of blank overhanging rock.

Dropping back to the top of the pedestal, I drank the last of my water and thought about Yosemite. My bright idea of a remote climb was losing its luster rapidly. I could picture my friends in the Valley, who had probably come down from their routes before the afternoon heat, and were now sitting in the restaurant with a drink or cavorting in Camp Four, the Yosemite climbers' camp. I, on the other hand, contemplated a cold night at 13,000 feet and an arduous descent in the morning.

After a brief rest, I clipped a sling into my highest piton and stood in it. The overhanging wall pushed me out, and after a futile effort to surmount it, I descended again. The sun was about to leave the face, and I knew that my best chance was to give it everything I had while the rock was still warm. This time I put the shortest possible loop into the piton so I could stand a bit higher than before. The headwall had a shallow vertical groove; and I worked, with my elbow pointed skyward, to secure an arm-lock between my inverted palm and shoulder. When I tried to move my free leg, I felt completely helpless, but I made one final attempt. Dangling from the overhang by the arm-lock, I pulled my foot away from the security of the loop and up onto the eye of the piton. The extra inches let me move the arm-lock higher. I was now out of balance, but very near a wide crack, and a desperate lunge took me high enough to jam a fist into the bottom of the crack.

Relief surged through me, as though a gun aimed at my head had just misfired. The danger was not entirely over, however; I knew that my adrenalin-stimulated strength would be short-lived. I continued up, fist-jamming thirty feet to a narrow ledge, and panted there for long minutes. The ledge traversed the steep headwall for a hundred feet and then connected with a chimney system. It was a lucky break; I wouldn't need to bivouac on the cliff if I could move efficiently in the minutes remaining before dark.

The day's harsh sunlight gave way to dusk, and in

the indirect light I could see into the shadowy north faces of an endless sea of peaks. It was a more rugged Sierra vista than I had ever known in summer. At my feet were alpine flowers; this very contrast of life and barren rock had let John Muir to call the range "the gentle wilderness."

All along the ledge yellow hulsea and purple polemonium were still in bloom. Sierra bighorn sheep depend on them as an important part of their summer diet. In Muir's day, the flowers might have been nibbled down to the roots. Weathered horns and ancient Indian hunting blinds attest to the fact that the bighorn, now a threatened species, once ranged as high as the very tops of most mountains along the crest. I could imagine a ram profiled on the summit ramparts only a hundred feet above me as I hurried along the ledge below.

Having reached the chimney, I climbed steadily with the pack suspended below me, and within minutes I was standing on the summit in the last rays of the sun. I would have liked to linger, but it was late. I scrambled toward the shadows of the north side, heading down the broken face toward a tiny meadow

Bighorn sheep in the High Sierra. Only a few hundred remain.

with a stream. An hour later, in the dark, I bent down for my first drink in many hours.

I had planned to stop by the stream for only a minute, then descend in the moonlight to the forest below, but after eating a package of freeze-dried hash mixed with cold water, I realized that my legs didn't want to support my body any longer. Without standing up again, I crawled into my half-bag. Though extremely fatigued, I lay sleepless for hours, still carried along by the forced awareness the day had demanded. I felt lucky to have made the climb and to have gotten down safely. I no longer envied the climbers loafing around the Yosemite campground. I was content where I was, alone under the stars on a clear night.

I set off again before dawn, walking through Little Lakes Valley toward the roadhead. After a single day high in the mountains, the well-used trail and established campsites seemed like civilization. At sunrise I reached the trailhead where my bicycle was cached and soon reveled in a 6000-foot down hill ride. From the floor of Owens Valley I had to climb again, struggling up a 3000-foot grade in desert heat that was already intense. I stopped half a dozen times to plunge my upper body into mountain streams. At nine that morning, less than twenty-four hours after starting up the trail toward Bear Creek Spire, I reached my car, with barely enough energy left to lift the light ten-speed inside.

A solo climb such as the one I had just made is not a logical extension of Yosemite technique, which stresses extending limits of ability while protected by equipment. Nor is solo climbing simply the means to an end, for there are far easier ways to reach summits. It is a form of private, heightened awareness—something that anyone who has spent time alone under stress can understand. What makes it different and desirable is doing so by choice.

3
The
Great
White
Throne

DURING the 1960s climbers who wanted to ascend the legendary sandstone towers of the American desert faced almost as many restrictions as travelers wishing to visit Tibet. Access to the best climbs was forbidden by either government agencies or the Navajo tribe, which, after a century of oppression, had begun to reassert itself. Visitors were required to pay a fee to enter reservation lands, and climbing was outlawed on the sacred cliffs of Monument Valley and Shiprock. The 2000-foot cliffs of Zion Canyon, in southern Utah, were also off-limits because of a ruling by the National Park Service. Although roped ascents of the easiest sides of the formations were permitted, attempts on the great walls had been banned; park rangers judged the soft sandstone unsafe for Yosemite-style sieges, during which climbers must live on a wall for days.

Fred Beckey was the most ubiquitous North American climber of the postwar era. The veteran of a thousand routes—mostly first ascents—Fred had a reputation for succeeding through persistence rather than by unusual skill. Difficulties that held back other

Opposite page:
The Great White Throne, northwest face.

23

climbers—trailless approaches, blank headwalls, miserable weather—seemed only to increase his determination. Fred wanted to climb the 2200-foot northwest face of the Great White Throne, Zion's most famous landmark. He first applied for permission in 1965 and was turned down, but this failed to deter him. Reasoning that bureaucracy thrives on a constant diet of paper, he began a stream of correspondence to the park service director, the regional office, the superintendent, the chief ranger, assorted secretaries, and undoubtedly a garbage collector or two. Each letter was duly and courteously answered, and Fred in turn would respond, *ad infinitum*. Ultimately, he wore down the agency's resistance, and special permission

Fred Beckey
sorting
equipment on the
Great White
Throne.

was granted on the conditions that the climbers maintain radio communication with the ground and have a rescue party available.

In early April of 1967 I joined Fred and Pat Callis in Zion. Our support party consisted of Pat's wife and Harry Woodworth, a friend of mine from California. Their job was to operate the ground radio and to call the Tacoma Mountain Rescue Team if necessary.

We were gratified to find firm rock on the cliffs at the bottom of the canyon. The same rock, Navajo sandstone, is found in varying degrees of hardness throughout the Southwest. During the Permian period, the Zion area was covered by an inland sea. When those waters retreated, one of the world's largest deserts began to form. For millions of years, however, the climate was still wet enough to leach iron oxide from the distant mountains. Great sand dunes covered the landscape, and sedimentary rock formed at their bases as calcium carbonate—lime—mixed with iron oxide to weld grains of sand together. Later on, the climate became drier; rain no longer washed iron oxide from the hills, and only pure carbonate glued the particles together.

The Great White Throne stood before us like a cross-sectional illustration in a textbook. Shaped like a brick standing on end, its lower third was fiery red, and the upper sections were whiter than Yosemite granite. At its base was the tiny Virgin River, which had cut two thousand feet through rock over eons of time. Smaller side streams had carved the other sides of the Throne, creating a monolith that stood independent of the other canyon walls. All the cliffs were striped in white and red bands, and we understood why the tourist brochures proclaimed Zion "Yosemite Valley in Color."

We didn't expect the quality of the rock to match the area's scenic beauty, but we were pleasantly surprised to begin the climb on firm rock with continuous cracks. On the first lead I protected a long lieback with several pitons driven as solidly as possible. Pat had trouble hammering them out, which increased our confidence in the rock's strength. Higher up I drilled two expansion bolts into crackless rock and found that it took nearly as long as it would have to drill into granite. We came down that evening, leaving fixed ropes up to our high point. The next day we reached a forested ledge in the center of the face late in the day. Since the weather had begun to look bad, we descended again.

A fast-moving cold front passed through that night, covering the mountains with snow, and we awoke to clearing skies in a fairyland of frosted sandcastles. Two days later we started our final push. Several hours of climbing brought us to our old high point, where Fred began leading a vertical crack using direct aid. The character of the rock changed abruptly. Gone was the hard red sandstone, and now we encountered gray rock that crumbled to pieces in our hands. Fred's pitons sank like nails driven into soft bark. When he could no longer make a piton hold his weight, he drilled a hole for an expansion bolt. The quarter-inch drill made a rounded pit big enough for his little finger. "This stuff is like brown sugar," he yelled down. "There's no way we can continue with the equipment we have."

Our afternoon radio call brought a forecast of a series of storms. We descended again and called a council of war. Apparently, the impure lime that held together the white sandstone of the upper cliffs was partly water soluble. The red rock was far more sound to begin with and relatively unaffected by the moisture. Fred had tried the old desert trick of drilled-in angles—driving a three-quarter-inch sawed-off piton into a quarter-inch drilled hole—but the sharp edges of the piton broke the rock away, and none of us felt safe trusting our lives to such devices. We decided to go home for a few weeks and return when the weather had stabilized and the rock was dry. I would make up a batch of new anchors that could be twisted into drilled holes where the rock was soft. Fred would monitor the weather and call us when the time was right.

I had the opportunity to observe one of Fred's

weather checks when he visited my automotive shop shortly after we returned to California. Never one to waste money, Fred used a pay phone to make a toll-free call to directory assistance in southern Utah. When the operator came on, he asked her what the weather was like. She replied that she didn't have that information and offered him the weather number. "No, no, I don't need that," Fred told her. "Just look out your window and tell me if there are any clouds. And is it windy? How warm is it? Operator? Operator?"

The operator hung up, but Fred patiently tried again and again, until he persuaded someone to look out the window. He repeated this process daily, and also checked the newspaper weather maps. It proved to be the worst spring in thirty years. The usual high pressure zone over the Great Basin never became established, and a battery of storms from the Pacific marched continuously inland.

Fred sounded the bugle at last in early May, and we met in Zion under clouds. With a prediction for clearing skies we returned to our high point, where Pat took over the lead on Fred's "brown-sugar" pitch. It was overcast and still as Pat climbed Fred's ladder of pitons, but as soon as he ventured onto new ground we witnessed the most sudden change in weather I had ever seen. Pat described his experience:

> The sky became dark and from far below came the wailing of a violent wind rushing up the canyon floor, bending the trees and whipping the water of the river. Lightning, thunder, and suddenly the air was full of swirling snow. I stood in my slings as though in a trance, fascinated and frightened by the swiftness with which the storm had transformed our world into a hostile place. The storm seemed to magnify the distance between my belayer and myself, and I felt alone and frail. Meekly, I retreated down the snow-choked crack in a puppet-like response to the beckoning of my companions.

In a matter of a few minutes, the fierce squall moved on; and the sun came out. Pat finished his lead, and I spent several hours working up a straight-forward crack with direct aid. Such a stretch could have been climbed in minutes on Yosemite granite. Tap a piton a couple of times; clip in the rope and a sling; stand higher; tap another. Here each piton placement had to be laboriously prepared. Sometimes I would beat on a piton for several minutes, only to have it fall out loosely in my hand. Then I would drive a bigger one into the slot. At best it took about a hundred hard bashes to drive a two-inch blade into a crack, and we were both exhausted by the end of the day. We rappelled four hundred feet and joined Fred in a camp with a fire on a spacious ledge.

The following day we hauled loads of food, equipment, and water up to "Last Chance Ledge," six hundred feet from the summit. Above lay the crux of the route. A curving open book stretched from the summit to about two hundred fifty feet above our ledge, but the area in between was overhanging and quite blank. We were gratified, though, to find thin cracks leading up the headwall. Fred and Pat spent the remainder of the day on two painfully slow leads. Fred just reached the open book as alpenglow turned the upper face into the color of a living ember.

We returned to Last Chance Ledge that night, and in the morning I went up to take the first lead. On the overhanging soft rock I had considerable trouble finding decent cracks for pitons. Fred persuaded me to use nylon loops tied around the inch-thick trunk of a decaying juniper that stuck out of a crack, claiming that any tree with greenery on it would hold a man's weight. I put a tie-off loop around the trunk, cautiously pulled on it, attached a sling, and stepped up. At first the tree held my weight—but just as Fred was telling me that the more I climbed, the more I would learn to trust trees that grew on cliffs, there was a loud snap. The tree broke off, and I flew through the air with it attached to the rope just above me. Fred's belay through a lower piton stopped me after a thirty-foot fall. Since the face was over-

Galen Rowell climbing in Yosemite in the same year as his ascent of the Great White Throne. Photo by Layton Kor.

hanging, I was unhurt, except where the tree slid down the rope and scratched me. I untied it and watched it fall the full distance to the desert floor below.

I tried the same spot again and took another fall when a soft foothold broke. On the third try I slowly drilled my way past the tree stump using lag screws. Three hundred feet of easier climbing put us on a big ledge near the top. The last lead went up steeply for fifteen feet, and we expected it to gradually round off onto the summit. At the top of the little headwall, our climb ended with stunning abruptness. One second I was over the big drop; the next I was walking on a plateau. By sunset we had all of the party and equipment on top.

We had never visited such a mountain summit. Inaccessible except by technical climbing, it was a level island of desert, half a mile wide. It had been reached only a few times by seven hundred feet of rockclimbing from the south side. Park rangers had told us a little about the natural history of this lofty mesa. A lightning fire here a few years back had been allowed to burn itself out, leaving the top more barren than the surrounding high desert plateau. Somehow, several species of mammals frequented the summit. One party had sighted a bobcat. We saw chipmunks during the day and a kangaroo rat at night. The scuffling sound of a larger animal near our fire led us to the tracks of a ringtail cat.

The top of the Throne was quite a liveable place except for the absence of water. Only small rodents, specially adapted to extracting liquid from their food, could live here year-round. We wondered how these animals, residents and visitors alike, had come here. One biologist has theorized that predatory birds carried up any rodents that now live on top. Although none of us had degrees in natural history, our experience led us to distrust complex solutions that ignored the obvious. We suspected that, rather than being airlifted, these animals had simply done as we had: climbed under their own power. Climbers in every part of the world have come back with unusual animal sightings. The *yeti* tracks found by Eric Shipton in the

Himalayan snows have yet to be satisfactorily explained, but there is little doubt, for example, that a large climbing party on Mount Rainier really did watch a black bear casually step onto the summit, turn around, and head back down the miles of crevassed glaciers. We all had seen rats high on Yosemite cliffs, even in the middle of El Capitan where crack systems didn't appear to connect.

In the morning we set up seven one-hundred-fifty-foot rappels to descend the back side. Reaching the main valley would have taken twenty more rappels, so we traversed across the high country toward a highway four miles away. Following heavily used deer trails over exposed sandstone, we could easily imagine a desperado behind every rock. At one spot that would have been perfect for a B-movie ambush, I came across a freshly killed deer and cat tracks as big as my fist angling toward a ravine. A mountain lion had made the kill and was probably watching us from a safe distance, waiting to return when we left.

The transition to civilization was as abrupt as reaching the summit had been. Around a corner, sage and trailless sandstone ran smack into a highway. That evening we were treated to a victory dinner by the only restaurant in the nearest town, and on the way out I passed Fred Beckey using the pay phone. "Anchorage information? What's the weather like up there? No, just look out your window . . ."

4
The
South
Face of
Half Dome

HALF DOME is not really half a dome. From every point in Yosemite Valley one sees the perfect image of its name, but viewed from the rear its true form becomes apparent. Instead of the rounded south wall one expects, there is a steep cliff, slightly higher and far more flawless than the famous front, or northwest, face. Half Dome actually is a whole dome with a character unlike any other dome in America.

Until 1870 geologists argued convincingly that Yosemite's cliffs had been formed by the bottom dropping out of the valley, and that Half Dome must have been whole until one side was sheared off in some primeval cataclysm. After John Muir studied Yosemite, however, he wrote that the "Master Builder" had chosen "not the earthquake nor lightning to rend and split asunder . . . but tender snowflowers falling noiselessly eon after eon, the offspring of the sun and the sea." Muir's glacial theory proved closer to the truth than the cataclysmic one, but modern geologists have discovered that the greater part of Half Dome was never glaciated. Ice gave the dome its clean

Opposite page:
Aerial view of the south face of Half Dome.

appearance by scouring debris from the base, but its basic form is the result of gradual processes that were well under way before the ice ages.

Half Dome can be likened more accurately to the last joint of a thumb than to the cleaved hemisphere the name suggests. The textures of its sides are as different as a thumbnail and fingerprint. The northwest face is laced with crack systems produced by vertical joints—lines of structural weakness—cast into the granite as it cooled. The incredibly smooth surface of the south face is due to the total absence of such joints. The northwest is shady and streaked with lichens; the south bakes all day in the sun.

I was introduced to the true character of the south face by Warren Harding, who had made first ascents of many of the biggest Yosemite faces. By 1965 the back side of Half Dome, unseen except from trails above the Valley, was the last major unclimbed cliff in the park. Warren invited me to join him on a winter reconnaissance that he hoped would lead to a full-scale attempt on the face later that year. We planned to scout a climbing route by observing where fresh snow demarked cracks and ledges on the face, but after a four-mile walk to the base, we found overselves staring a vertical desert. No snow clung to the wall. It was featureless except for a single overhanging arch that ended in blankness.

Though Warren and I suspected that the south face might be the smoothest big cliff in the world, we never imagined that the ascent would ultimately require six attempts spread over five years—more actual climbing time than any of the dozen Himalayan or Alaskan climbs I've taken part in since. It was also an ascent that violated many of mountaineering's unwritten rules about style and technique. Climbs considered classics are rarely the most difficult routes but rather are ones that follow unexpected geologic weaknesses through seemingly impregnable terrain. The climber's joy in a classic first ascent has much in common with that of the research scientist who has made a ground-breaking discovery: it rests chiefly in the "elegance" of finding a simple solution to a complex

*Opposite page:
Galen Rowell
near the top of
the Great Arch
on the south face.
Photo by Warren
Harding.*

problem. To preserve this experience, climbers have generally agreed that drilling ladders of bolts is justified only to connect natural weaknesses, not as a major element of an ascent.

Warren never believed in following a prescribed ethic; he thought each person should choose his or her own brand of mountain madness. He had used one hundred bolts on otherwise unclimbable sections of the first route up El Capitan in 1958, and he estimated that one hundred fifty or so might be needed on the south face of Half Dome. We both considered this technique justified in making the first route up an especially blank wall.

On the first attempt in June 1966, we were joined by Yvon Chouinard and Chuck Pratt. After a close look at the face's terrible smoothness, Chouinard wanted to withdraw—not because of the difficulty but because of his dislike for the amount of artificial aid that would be needed. He stayed for the first pitch, during which he took a short fall, complained of an injured shoulder, and quit. A week later, with Gary Colliver along, we made another attempt. Gary rappelled down after one bivouac, but Warren and I continued on for three more days, following a crack system on the underside of the great arch. We felt as though we were ascending the inside of a 900-foot peaked roof. Our reward for surmounting this obstacle was a two-day wait in a storm, hanging inside an eighteen-inch slot. At the end of this ordeal Warren was still eager to go on, but it was now my turn to plead the cause of retreat on the grounds of a bad cold. We made no further attempts on the south face that year.

Warren's work kept him out of the country for the next year. When he returned, he began designing his now-legendary "Bat" equipment—the acronym stands for Basically Absurd Technology—for another go at the south face. Our living quarters would be Bat tents: single-point suspension, one-person, fully enclosed, semi-waterproof hammocks. Our progress over blank rock would be speeded by the use of Bat-hooks, tiny steel hooks that could be wedged into holes only one-third the depth required for bolts.

Even the name Warren Harding was no longer distinctive enough for the inventor of the Bat gadgets; Warren rechristened himself "Batso."

As we studied photo blow-ups of the face, the ascent began to take on an aura of fantasy. The dome itself resembled a giant bald head; its most obvious features were three closely spaced black spots that we named the Tri-clops Eye. Above this strange triple eye was a zone of darker rock that became known as the Gray Matter. Warren fantasized that the Tri-clops Eye was the entrance to a huge amphitheater in the center of the dome. When we reached it, we would be able to peer inside and see all the gods of the ancients seated around a table. Janus, the two-headed god of doorways, would be on hand to say, "Come in—we've been expecting you!"

In November 1968, after five days of climbing and fifty Bathooks drilled into flawless rock, Warren and I reached the right-hand eye of the Tri-clops. Our imaginary amphitheater vanished in the face of reality: we found neither cave nor ledge—in fact, barely a dent in the armorplate. The reality proved exciting enough, however. As we set up our Bat tents for yet another night on the face, nature was changing the sets in preparation for a wild scene. Cirrus clouds raced by overhead, billowing cumulus hung over the High Sierra to the east, and a seething, sporadically moving mass of cloud oozed up from the floor of the canyon below. Darkness and the white mass overcame us simultaneously. At midnight we were awakened by raindrops, at four it began snowing, and by dawn everything was white.

Peering outside our Bat tents, we saw that our vertical wall was plastered with a thick layer of wet snow. As the day warmed, we witnessed a striking demonstration of how the Tri-clops were formed. They were focal points for drainage on the upper wall. Soon both of us were in the middle of a temporary waterfall and soaked to the skin. The hours came and went with painful slowness. Our Bat tents were indeed watertight: water seeped in where they touched the rock, but it didn't seep out. Our sleeping bags became thin bags of nylon with lumps of wet goose

down coagulated near the bottom. We punctured
holes in the floor of the tents for drainage, shivered
continuously, and prayed for sun. At noon we con-
ferred via small walkie-talkies with our support party
on the trail to the south of us, and were advised that
no major storm was forecast. Assuming our weather
to be a local disturbance, we decided to wait it out,
while our friends walked down to the Valley in the
rain.

Small avalanches struck us as we hung motionless. Fingers and toes numbed, and our skin became as
wrinkled as a prune. After another night and morning passed, the air grew colder and still the storm continued. Warren wanted to stay, but I wanted to descend. I didn't want to die without a fight, and the
choices seemed absurdly clear: November snow,
hypothermia, and frostbite versus a warm fire and a
filet mignon dinner. Finally I yelled over the howling
wind, "Warren, we have to go down!"

Warren Harding
peering out of a
Bat tent on Half
Dome.

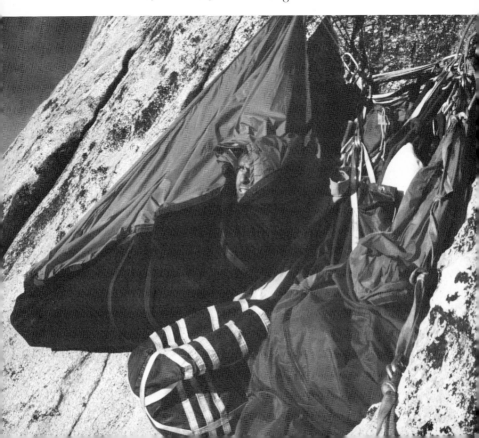

"We?" came the answer. "I've played that game before, and I'm not moving anywhere."

I pouted for a while, and, considering the odds of freezing if I stayed, decided to descend alone. I figured that it would take about ten rappels with a doubled rope which I would have to pull down by one end after each descent in order to set up the following rappel. I said goodbye to Warren and promised him help as soon as I reached the Valley. Disappearing down the wall, I realized that I would need to swing across the face for a few feet in order to reach the next anchor point. Eight feet below the Tri-clops, however, I discovered that I couldn't move out of the plumb line of the rope. The rock was coated with ice, and further testing showed that the rappel rope was frozen in place at the top and wouldn't pull down.

I was in a far more serious position than the one I had just left above in the Tri-clops eye. Constant powder avalanches knocked me about and filled my supposedly waterproof clothing. I became infinitely cold, and my thoughts went from down to up, to the comparative safety of the bivouac. My mechanical ascenders wouldn't work on the icy rope; I tied special prusik knots so I could climb the rope. They held, but instead of sliding, they froze in place. My hands became immobile clubs, and I constantly fought blacking out as I neared the top. I yelled up to Warren to tie all our nylon loops together and lower them, but they reached only twenty feet. Dizziness overwhelmed me, and I didn't think I could make it. At long last I reached the loops and climbed the icy rope ladder to the Bat tents. They seemed much warmer—and Warren much smarter—than they had two hours earlier.

Hours later a faint yell from the base of the face signaled a radio call. For the first time in his life, Warren Harding asked for assistance: "We're not doing very well. We're wet, cold, and a little numb. Get us off if you can!" Our friends rushed down to the Valley and returned hours later with a terse message: "Helicopter . . . on . . summit . . . two . . . hours." Then all was silent. Moisture had taken its toll on our cheap electronics.

Hours passed, and the sun set under a mantle of clouds. Suddenly a helicopter flew by, then made several passes. Our hopes soared, then dropped to a new low as the sky once more grew dark and silent. We knew that the helicopter couldn't fly near the cliff at night, so we concentrated on just surviving the agonizing cold. Long after dark we were startled by a strange, squawking noise. Then a light shone down the cliff, illuminating a man with a headlamp, radio, and heavy clothing being lowered on the end of a rope. Unseen by us, the helicopter had been shuttling people and equipment to the summit of Half Dome. The man on the rope was Royal Robbins, descending like a guardian angel to bring us hot soup, dry parkas and gloves, and a lifeline to the summit. We started to warm up as we climbed the eight-hundred-foot rope with jumar ascenders, and by midnight we were on top in a spacious tent with dry cloths, warm drinks, and old friends.

Four months later, in March 1969, Warren and I recovered our unique and expensive equipment by climbing the tourist route on the northeast side of the dome and then rappelling down to the Tri-clops Eye. We planned to give the face another go later that spring, but melting snow from the heaviest Sierra winter on record followed by Warren's commitment to a construction project kept us away. Warren notified his boss that he planned to take time off in September to resume our climb, but fate took another nasty turn. On the afternoon of his last day on the job, Warren's thoughts were thousands of feet above the central California highway project. He walked squarely into the path of a fast-moving truck, and his leg was crushed. For weeks the doctors didn't know if he would walk again, much less climb. But a series of operations reconnected ligaments and pinned shattered bones, and by December he was hobbling around on crutches and telling me: "May. We'll go back and do it this time."

Joe Faint had helped us recover our gear the previous winter, and he wanted to take part in the next attempt. On a sunny June day the three of us hiked to the base. I knew Warren was going to do fine when he limped past me with the heaviest pack. No sooner had we roped up for the first pitch, then the sky turned ominous. It was our fourth storm in four attempts, and Joe began talking about omens. After our first bivouac, the weather was still threatening; and he suddenly wanted nothing more to do with the climb. We descended but were caught in a downpour before we reached the base. "Those who fail to heed the lessons of history are doomed to repeat them," Joe told us with finality. (We learned the next day that he was offering all his climbing equipment for sale.)

Several days later, on a clear morning, Warren and I returned. True to form, it began to snow before we had climbed the four hundred feet of fixed rope back to our previous high point. With undiminished confidence—and plastic covers for our Bat tents—we resolved to wait out the weather. But as I stepped out of my tent to get some food from a haul bag, the sky lit up for a split second before the earth shook. The lightning gave me a strong jolt, sending me reeling against my anchor sling. Once I had recovered my wits, I figured out what had happened. When lightning strikes a cliff, electricity flows along cracks and flaws in the rock, and although we were on the least-flawed piece of rock in America, it did have one: the nine-hundred-foot crack in the arch that we were hanging from. The storm continued for two days. We tried to climb anyway, but got soaked in a small waterfall that crossed our route. On day three we descended.

On the first day of our sixth attempt, in July, yet another rainstorm hit us. It stopped as we continued to climb, however, and on the third day we reached our familiar high point in the Tri-clops Eye. The plastic water bottles we had filled in the Merced River four years earlier still dangled from the anchor bolts; we added purifier to the water and drank heartily. The weather stayed blessedly clear for two more days, as we climbed up a two-hundred-foot blank headwall and into the thin cracks of the Gray Matter. On the third night's bivouac we hung our hammocks under a

small overhang, not knowing whether we were one hundred or four hundred feet from the top.

Clouds moved across the sky all night long, and we awoke under total overcast at 5:30 a.m. I began a lead that consisted mainly of drilling and ended in blankness just before noon; then I broke out my Bat tent for the inevitable storm. I didn't want to think about the possibility that we might be forced down again, this close to the top. Raindrops fell as Warren donned his parka and started drilling up a black water streak that we had hoped might be a crack. The rock had a peculiar porcelain-like quality, as though it had been fired in a kiln, and was so hard that drilling took twice the normal time. For hour after hour the light drizzle threatened to worsen. I fed Warren all the rope, and he asked for more. Just as I gave him the last coil tied to my waist, he yelled, "Off belay! I'm up!"

As I climbed the rope to join Warren on the summit, a swift flew between us, unconcerned and unimpressed by our accomplishment. The fact that we had managed to falter our way through Half Dome's southern defenses had done little to change the formidable nature of the face. I remembered John Muir's words of exactly a century earlier, two years before a Scot named George Anderson drilled his way up the gentle slabs where cables now guide visitors: "The dome . . . would hardly be more 'conquered' or spoiled should man be added to her list of visitors. His louder screams and heavier scrambling would not stir a line of her countenance."

Opposite page:
Warren Harding
at the top of the
Great Arch.

5
The
Seventh
Rifle

DAWN ARRIVED, but no sunrise accompanied it. A veil of autumn snow filtered from the sky, settling on the limbs of trees and on the blankets of the men who slept in the clearing. One man was awake, building a fire. Next to him, camouflaged by the white sky and falling snow, lay the fresh skin and feet of a mountain goat; nearby were the dim shapes of ten live horses and three dead grizzly bears. Under the trees lay an assortment of equipment, including a theodolite, several rifles, an immense camera, and an ice axe.

The year was 1910, and the setting was the Bugaboo Mountains of British Columbia. As I watched this imaginary scene out of the past, the sleeping men arose and joined their comrade by the fire. They talked of surveying and picture-taking, and of animals and shots they had missed with their rifles. They spoke of shooting at grouse, squirrels, deer, a bear cub. I wanted to jump in among them and say, "Look here! Have some respect for those animals! They have as much right to be here as you. And killing all those grizzlies—they're becoming scarce, you know."

Opposite page: Tony Qamar leading on the second morning, west face of North Howser Tower, Bugaboo Mountains, British Columbia.

45

But this was sheer fancy, removed as I was by some sixty years and six thousand feet from that September morning scene. I was also pioneering, halfway up the 3300-foot face of North Howser Tower. My eyes were focused on a spot in a forested canyon more than a mile below me, and my gaze had not wavered for a long time. I wondered if I was looking at the spot where those men, the first Bugaboo climbers, had camped over half a century before.

At my back was a virgin granite wall; below me was some of the wildest country I had ever seen. In the whole vast panorama I could see no trace of a trail, a road, or other evidence of man, yet the image of that 1910 survey party intruded on my impression of an untouched wilderness. The current of evolution had been interrupted, however slightly, by early visitors with the pioneer ethic and lots of ammunition. More disturbing still was the realization that had I been alive in 1910 and sitting around the campfire with six men, ten horses, dead goats, grizzlies, and grouse, I would not have questioned their ethics. There would have been a seventh rifle leaning against the tree.

I started as though waking from a dream, but I had not been sleeping. It took me a moment to notice that the evening wind had blown out the camp stove at my side, and slowly I became conscious of the other details of my surroundings. I was alone on a ledge, 1500 feet above a glacier. Above me, my climbing partners, Chris Jones and Tony Qamar, were fixing a rope. The ledge was strewn with equipment: bright blue sleeping bags, red jackets, orange jackets, various colors of polyethylene rain gear, freeze-dried food, jumar ascenders, a Bleuet stove cartridge, a bolt kit, and two ice axes. Except for the last item, how foreign it all would have seemed to Conrad Kain, the man by my daydream campfire.

The 1910 scene in the clearing I had recalled from a description in Kain's memoirs. The first mountaineer to explore the Bugaboo Range, he was also first to climb the highest of the Howser Towers the peak whose west face we were now climbing. If

Kain were alive today, he would be in his late eighties, about as old as my father. I could hardly believe that people of his generation, born in the age of muskets, before the advent of the automobile, were still alive in the age of the hydrogen bomb and space travel.

Our climb seemed to bridge that time span—it was technical in a limited sense, yet primitive—still wild, but only a long day's walk from civilization. We were carrying a bare minimum of equipment; if we succeeded, it would not be because we had carried all the "right" gear, as many advertisers would have one believe. On the contrary, it was the absence of items often considered essential that enabled us to move quickly in alpine rather than Himalayan style—climbing in one push without moving up and down fixed ropes between established camps on the face.

It felt satisfying to be doing a big wall in this "ethical" style. But climbing ethics are rarely as lofty as they seem. Often they are merely the ethics of convenience. For instance, British climbers began using nuts for protection, not because they saved the rock from damage—which has become the modern rationale—but because local rock was well-suited to them. Americans began to remove pitons en route not for

Chris Jones and Judy Sterner approaching the Howser Towers from the east.

montane esthetics but because they were heavy and costly. A climb like the Howser Tower might require ten pitons on each of thirty rope leads. This would mean carrying three hundred pitons that would weigh about seventy-five pounds and cost about $600. By recovering them as the last man came up, we were able to get by with a collection of only twenty pitons and a few nuts. On the low cliffs of England, or the less technically demanding climbs of the Alps, however, it made perfect sense for the first ascent party to leave its hardware in place. But now we were moving quickly and carrying as little gear as possible because heavy hauling is hard work; because the less time spent, the lower the odds of being caught by a storm; and because keeping my family in a motel in the nearest town was expensive.

Fixed ropes, placing bolts, and step-cutting in ice have all been called unethical by modern climbers. Doing without such techniques is indeed bolder, but it is also faster and less strenuous than the old-fashioned methods. Behind the mask of courage and style, the masters of modern techniques still follow the ethics of convenience.

Our three-man system moved us up the face efficiently, in much the same manner that the jerky, opposing motions inside an engine deliver a constant flow of power in one direction. Compared to the normal alternation of two climbers on a wall, our system allowed for only minimal rest time. After a lead was completed, the second climber jumared up immediately to take over the lead, while the third cleaned the hardware and tied on the loads to be hauled up. Pitch after pitch flashed by as we leapfrogged in this way over mixed terrain.

Chris kicked steps up a snow patch; I slithered over a wet overhang; Tony frisked past an awkward headwall. The holes in the knees of my 69¢ U.S. Air Force tropical blues gaped to the wind after a difficult jam crack. By lunch on the second day we couldn't count the pitches we had climbed in the morning. As we nibbled on salami and cheese, a bald eagle glided past and landed on a rock gendarme. Without ac-

Opposite page: The 3300-foot west face of North Howser Tower.

knowledging our presence, the great bird soared on, then turned in a circle over the glacier and flew between our towers. An earlier generation might have taken that as an omen; as we watched the bird disappear, we thought of how it was an animal counterpart of a B-52 on a combat mission.

I began to gauge our progress by carving imaginary notches on the ridge of the adjoining South Tower. Following the ridge downward with my eyes until it ended on a snowy shelf, I spotted the black boulder under which forty man-days of food had been cached by an earlier expedition that had been forced off the face by bad weather. Having obtained their permission before our climb, we had feasted on canned bacon, hotcakes, and Trappist Monk brandy jelly—another benefit of coming sixty years after Conrad Kain.

As the sun set under a cloud bank, we traversed the final, knife-edged ridge to the summit. We bivouacked just below the top and found the morning air alarmingly warm. As we descended via the easier east face route, the bergschrund groaned repeatedly, and moments after I reached the glacier and stood clear of the steep wall, a wet snow avalanche erased my tracks behind me. Tony finished the last rappel and made new tracks rather more quickly.

After pulling out our camp at the base, we reached Boulder Camp, four miles from the roadhead, late in the afternoon. We experienced a strong dose of culture shock, for where generations of climbers had found only wildflowers and waterfalls, we were treated to the sight of two new huts erected by the Alpine Club of Canada—white plastic hemispheres capped with red ventilators. These dwellings housed a gaggle of guides, cooks, and clients on the main floor, and the basements were occupied by noisy families of super ground squirrels. These rodents, termed "snafflehounds" because of their propensity for theft, had become a master race with a gene pool that changed far more rapidly than under natural conditions. The slow and unwary were shot with a guide's rifle as they free-climbed up the hardest boulders toward food or snaffle-prusiked up ropes toward suspended bags; in consequence, the survivors displayed considerably more speed, cunning, and wits than their primate cohabitants. To our dismay, we learned that the Alpine Club planned to move one of the huts to the west side of the Howser Towers, blasting a platform with dynamite if necessary. A newer, multistory hut would be built in Boulder Camp.

On a previous trip I had stayed in antique cabins at the roadhead. We now found them gone, and nearby the new Bugaboo Lodge graced a clearing below the toe of the glacier. The interior proved to be a tasteful blend of the Old World and the modern, yet I felt vaguely uneasy. I picked up a brochure bearing a picture of a helicopter hovering over the Bugaboos and the caption, "Conquer the High Country by Helicopter!" A sign innocently asked us to remove mountain boots before going upstairs, a ritual that defined our arrival in civilization.

My uneasiness gradually became fathomable. Had the Bugaboo Lodge been in town instead of near the foot of the glacier I would have welcomed its comforts with open arms. Now that the climb was over I had little desire to remain in the mountains. Kain had once stayed comfortable for months in the Bugaboo high country by carrying in enough equipment to live simply off the land. We had managed with far less gear while in the mountains, but always at hand was the prospect of a fast return to civilization. This was my "seventh rifle"—not actually leaning against a tree like Kain's but always part of my mental arsenal.

When Kain had returned from the Bugaboos six decades before, he hiked out thirty miles further to reach civilization and wrote in his diary: "It was pleasant to see a covered table once more and a good bed with sheets. But I could not sleep—it was too soft and comfortable."

6
A Winter Traverse of the White Mountains

THE SOUND began as a low roar far up the canyon. Then it shrieked, groaned, and tore its way out of the sky as if a giant object were falling. Powerless, we braced ourselves for the inevitable shock. Out of the darkness it came: the headlong, invisible charge of the wind. Our tent leaned, twisted, stretched, and flapped, until it seemed no longer anchored to the ground. Then, suddenly, all was still again, except for the whisper of falling snow and the anxious, uneven breathing of the four men inside the tiny shelter.

For four days and five nights we sat out the biggest winter storm of 1974 in our camp at 10,000 feet in the White Mountains of California. Winds of more than one hundred miles per hour, we learned later, had ripped the ice from the surface of a large lake twenty miles to the west. During a lull near the end of the storm, we skied to a grove of lodgepole pines in search of wood for a warming and drying fire. We found a healthy tree more than two feet in diameter that had been freshly broken—snapped off ten feet above the base. The broken piece, which must have

Opposite page: Descending to the Patriarch Grove of bristlecone pines, White Mountains, California.

53

weighed tons, had been carried thirty feet by the wind without leaving a single mark in the snow.

It was February 1974; the four of us were attempting the first winter traverse of the eighty-mile-long crest of the White Mountains. Paralleling the Sierra on the east side of the Owens Valley, these arid mountains have few trees, no lakes, very few fishing streams, and a Great Basin climate, with recorded temperatures reaching as low as $-38°$ F. Pellisier Flats, an eight-mile-long plateau at 13,000 feet, freezes every month of the year and has real arctic tundra. The crest of the range averages over 12,000 feet. Miles of treeless highlands are exposed to relentless west winds. During the Pleistocene epoch, these winds blew so much snow to the lee side of the crest that glaciers formed in cirques above what is now the Nevada desert.

That same wind, not the steepness or the cold, was now our adversary. When we saw the storm coming on the fifth day of our trip, we descended toward timberline to about 10,000 feet. On the crest there was nowhere to hide from the relentless wind—no trees, caves, or natural windbreaks of any kind. At night our survival had depended totally on our four-man tent, which the manufacturer had personally assured us was the most wind-stable on the market. It was cozy inside, but from the outside, especially at night and with a light glowing from within, it seemed as fragile as a butterfly's wing. If the wind had ripped open a seam, we would have been rudely thrust into the arctic night.

As desolate as these mountains seemed, we were not alone. Although humans had yet to traverse the range in winter, we found surprising evidence of animals living at this unfriendly altitude. At 13,400 feet we had a rare encounter with a band of five desert bighorn sheep. At nearly 14,000 feet, tracks of coyotes and white-tailed jackrabbits made crazy, interlocking patterns in the snow. On a cache trip up a side canyon, one of us had seen a cougar at close range. And most surprising was a lone mustang standing on a bluff—at 10,000 feet in the middle of a blizzard.

*Opposite page:
Camp on the
California-
Nevada border
below summit of
Boundary Peak
(13,140 feet).*

Our foursome was a most unlikely group of adventurers; an ex-auto mechanic, two carpenters, and a sewer-line worker. Jay Jensen and George Miller, the two carpenters, lived in Bishop, California, a small town in the Owens Valley at the base of the White Mountains. Both had been introduced to wilderness adventures by Dave Sharp, the sewer-line worker, who had once been their high school teacher. Dave had an enviable winter job: making snow surveys on skis across roadless Sierra passes for the state of California. I was the ex-auto mechanic, and for me the Owens Valley had become a second home. For many years while I still owned a business in the San Francisco Bay Area, I frequently drove a thousand miles in one weekend to spend time there. However different our backgrounds, we all shared a deep attachment to exploring these desert peaks.

This trip climaxed many earlier visits to the White Mountains. George, Jay, and three friends had previously attempted a winter traverse of the crest in 1973. By the fifth day of that trip, they had covered less than a third of the total distance. Some eighteen inches of new snow had fallen, and they decided to dig a snow cave rather than risk pitching a tent in high wind at 13,200 feet. As usual in the Whites, they found the windblown snow very shallow; they were compelled to dig into a hillside and to build the cave on two levels with a low roof only two feet thick. At 3 a.m. Jay awoke with a sensation of being smothered. The roof was closer to his head than it had been; there was not enough light to see his hands in front of his eyes, and he began to feel panicky. The cave was starting to collapse. Quickly waking the others, he crawled outside into a sixty-mile-an-hour wind and blizzard conditions. Putting up a tent was out of the question; some of the group couldn't even find their boots. Those who could locate theirs frantically dug a small alcove near the door of the cave, then tried to protect the entrance with the unfolded tent. Spindrift blew steadily inside; and gradually, over a twenty-minute period, the old part of the cave collapsed. The tiny alcove began to fill with snow.

Blindly, they fumbled into boots, gloves, and skis, and took off toward lower elevations. Within a few feet of the cave, George set off a small avalanche but rode it out safely. A few hours later, on descending as far as a subsidiary ridgetop at 11,000 feet, they found clear weather; above them the crest was still in storm. The summits didn't come out of the clouds until fourteen days after they gave up.

The present trip had been planned more carefully. Realizing the seriousness of any equipment failure, we began with new, identical packs, gaiters, skis, bindings, and poles. The exception was George, who insisted on trying thinner, lighter skis. A month before the trip, we had spent three days skiing up a side canyon to place a food cache on the crest. A second cache was flown in to the only permanent residence on the crest of the Whites, the University of California Barcroft Research Laboratory. At 12,470 feet, this facility is the highest year-round dwelling in the United States, supplied for more than half the year only by helicopter. Normally the lab discourages visitors, but we had obtained special permission to leave the cache.

But even careful planning can't anticipate the weather, and when the storm finally ended in its fourth day, we weren't sure how to proceed. The day before the storm began, we had reached the first cache and picked up a six-day supply of food; we now had two days' worth left. Some of us thought we should return to the cache—a full day's round trip— and pick up an extra margin of food for the 15-mile journey over the top of White Mountain Peak to the Barcroft lab. George suggested abandoning the effort altogether in favor of taking a ski run into Nevada, and then hitchhiking to a hot spring for a long soak. At last, however, we decided to go for it with only our less-than-ample provisions.

The morning after the storm ended was perfectly clear. In sub-zero temperatures we broke trail through deep snow; and by noon were back on the crest, enjoying the sun and the novelty of a rare windless day. Eye-to-eye with the peaks of the High Sierra across the 11,000-foot chasm of Owens Valley, we

Dave Sharp in deep snow on White Mountain Peak's summit ridge.

seemed to be far above the earth, skiing in the floating clouds. To the north, one hundred fifty miles away, we could see Mount Rose fading into the horizon. To the south, we looked past Mount Whitney to where the declining skyline of the Sierra merged with desert haze. Late in the day we arrived at a col at 13,400 feet. It was a strange place where some of the cornices, unlike those at our other camps, faced west instead of east. That evening we discovered why. Violent eddies of wind tried to rip the tent from its moorings, and we barely slept.

The next morning was still clear, and after an hour's skiing we reached the north ridge of White Mountain Peak—a granite knife-edge plastered with rime ice, with a drop of thousands of feet on either side. Tying our skis to our packs, we inched along the ridge through high winds and blowing snow, arriving at the summit around lunchtime. At 14,246 feet, White Mountain Peak was the highest point of our trip. The snow on the summit pyramid was glazed and wind-packed, and I was very glad to have metal edges on my skis for the steep run down the back side. The first mile went very quickly, but we soon reached an unskiable plateau where thousands of small rocks poked through the shallow snow. Barcroft Lab was still four long miles away. Some of us walked and others kept their skis on, stepping carefully through the rocks, trying to avoid the frequent grating noises. Late in the day, totally out of food and with the sky promising another storm, we finally reached the lab.

Our eleventh night in the mountains was very different from the first ten. We ate steaks, took showers, and walked around in T-shirts, perfectly warm. Upstairs in the two-story Quonset hut, we found the nation's highest library and its highest pool table, both in the same room. The library contained some rare nineteenth-century books on mountaineering and exploration. Reading them there, with the bitter cold blowing against the walls, lent a special significance to the historic adventures. The big storm that had trapped us in our tent had also damaged the power lines to the lab, and it was operating on emergency power from an ancient diesel generator. Mechanical failures were frequent; lights flickered, and the generator room took on the appearance of the hold of a leaking ship as hoses burst and workmen waded through a mixture of water and grease.

We spent two days waiting out the new storm: playing pool, reading, repairing ski bases, and watching the lab's resident mice and chickens. Its facilities were amazingly complete. Much high-altitude and space research has taken place in this tiny building which resembles an Antarctic outpost more than it does a California laboratory.

The next morning we were off again, stepping from the warmth of the lab onto snow that squeaked underfoot. For miles we followed treeless highlands, imperceptibly descending a thousand feet toward a gentle meeting with timberline. Not far from here a friend of mine had sat around a fire with a scientist named Edmund Schulman on a cool September evening in the 1950s. As the two men warmed their hands, Schulman pulled a brand from the fire and examined it closely. "1277 to 1283 A.D.," my friend recalls him saying. "This six-year ring pattern never repeats itself." When he had finished studying the flame-blackened ring pattern, he tossed the wood back into the fire. It burned long and hot and even.

Not long after that, Schulman became famous for his discovery that bristlecone pines are the oldest living things in the world. He never enjoyed his fame, however; he died before the publication of his most important work. History remembers Schulman as a practical scientist who proved with numbers and graphs that some bristlecones of the White Mountains are more than 4000 years old. My friend remembers Schulman as a man who lived in the wilderness of logic, seeking patterns in what appeared random—a man whose thoughts often wandered along loosely structured, mystical pathways. Already ill with heart disease in his forties, Schulman could not fail to note the contrast between the bristlecones and his own tenuous claim on life.

Even in his wildest dreams, however, Schulman never imagined the far-reaching effects of his discovery: that the twisted trees of the White Mountains would bring about a revolution in the study of Old World prehistory. Archaeologists formerly had dated European artifacts by the carbon-14 method; but Schulman's tree-ring chronology disagreed with carbon-14 datings of the wood—sometimes by as much as a thousand years. When the debate was finally settled, the bristlecones had won. A new bristlecone-corrected carbon-14 dating system came into being, which proved that artifacts of European culture were actually older than their supposed Mediterranean progenitors. The theory of cultural diffusion, which held that European culture was derived from the earlier civilizations of Egypt and Mesopotamia, was no longer valid.

Schulman had visited the bristlecones when the snow was gone and the trees rose naked from rocky ground. We saw them in quite a different setting, approaching on skis through an open forest clothed in white. The Patriarch Grove resembled a giant stage occupied by a troupe of frozen dancers; each tree seemed involved in the same motion, caught in pirouette, limbs extended. The west wind had shaped them and coated them with fingers of ice. They seemed to point toward some distant force in the sky.

We camped on the edge of the grove, watching sunrise color ancient bristlecone limbs while a full moon touched the horizon of the distant Sierra. It seemed a sacrilege even to hang our sleeping bags to dry on those trees. Each of us ran his hands over their wood, feeling the sensual warmth of a living thing that was already old in the winters of 1492 and 1776. Compared to these trees, we were a renewable resource.

That evening, sixteen days after we had begun the traverse, we reached Westguard Pass at the south end of the range. Our thoughts were still on the heights as we returned to a much younger world in the valley below.

7
Yosemite's Other Valley

THE TALE of Hetch Hetchy Valley resembles a Greek tragedy, but with a place instead of a person at its center. In the beginning there was a perfect half-scale version of Yosemite Valley, discovered by white men a year before they first entered Yosemite itself. While the larger valley soon bathed in international renown, Hetch Hetchy was being prepared for a different kind of bath. It was to become a reservoir. The final scene featured a star-studded cast that included John Muir, Woodrow Wilson, Gifford Pinchot, the Sierra Club, and most of the population of San Francisco.

As in all tragedies, the entire cast made out rather poorly in the end. Between President Wilson's signing of the fateful Raker Act, which permitted the long-fought Hetch Hetchy Dam to be built, and the actual drowning of the valley, both Wilson and Muir had died. Pinchot, undeniably a brilliant and conscientious man, would become infamous in environmental history for his support of a dam within a national park. Although Muir and the Sierra Club lost the battle, the city of San Francisco ended up with

Opposite page: Wapama Rock: Hetch Hetchy's El Capitan, Yosemite National Park.

only half a plum: through a strange contract, Hetch Hetchy power is sold to the Pacific Gas and Electric Company before it reaches the city, and PG&E then delivers it to the consumer—at a huge profit.

Once the dam's work was done, Hetch Hetchy entered a kind of limbo. The promised recreational facilities never appeared on its steep shoreline, and for most of this century it seemed that the valley's sole use—other than for water and power—was as a propaganda tool against future wilderness encroachments. Countless old Sierra Club Bulletins are sprinkled with references to the tragedy:

"What is Hetch Hetchy now? Just another damned artificial lake."

"Hetch Hetchy now isn't worth a 35mm Kodachrome film."

". . . nothing but a narrow body of monotonous water with an ugly shoreline surrounded by stark stone walls."

"Why should anyone go to Hetch Hetchy now?"

Thus admonished, conservationists shunned Hetch Hetchy. Even climbers ignored the place, generally supposing that access to its superb walls was not possible without a boat. Since boats are not allowed on the reservoir, and since swimming with a load of climbing equipment is rather difficult, the "stark stone walls" remain untouched as late as 1969.

In the spring of that year Joe Faint and I made the first major rock climb in Hetch Hetchy: the 1400-foot face of Wapama Rock, the counterpart of Yosemite's El Capitan both in appearance and geographical situation. The approach to the face was a surprisingly pleasant two-mile trail that meandered along a wide glacial bench directly below the cliffs. The bench itself seemed little affected by human travel, and the ugly shoreline was not visible unless one walked to the edge of the bench and peered down. Over glacier-scoured granite, through streams, meadows, and wildflowers, the trail delivered us to a point midway between two Yosemite-scale waterfalls. Two days later we reached the summit of the rock, but the main event of the climb was not reaching the top, it was the change in our attitude toward Hetch Hetchy. We had started the climb with a feeling of who-cares-what-they've-done-to-the-valley-we're-just-going-to-climb-the-rocks; we finished it with a new sense of the meaning of wildness.

It began with a nightmare. We had bivouacked on a sidewalk-wide ledge about halfway up the rock. Just before dawn I had been dreaming about sleeping on a ledge and slipping very close to the edge, but I wasn't worried because I was convinced that I was tied in. Then, still in the dream, I rolled over the edge, powerless to do anything but wait for the rope to stop me. It didn't, and I fell through the air for seconds— or perhaps minutes. I awoke with a start to find myself in reality very near the edge but reassuringly tight against the anchor rope. I peered through the pre-dawn haze at the imposing cliffs across the valley; still befuddled, I thought for a moment that I was on a climb in Yosemite Valley. It was the look down that turned my ideas about Hetch Hetchy onto a different track.

There lay the valley floor. But I saw no roads, no buildings, no campfires or smoke; heard no horns, motors, or voices. Below me was only a "narrow body of monotonous water," whereas if I had been in Yosemite Valley, the same site would have been occupied by Curry Village, fifty motor homes, a dozen tour buses, and the Valley tram car—all the dubious benefits of national park status. As the amber glow of the morning sun came creeping down the wall, we ate breakfast on our tiny ledge—a far cry from Yosemite Lodge, with its comfort, hot food, and Early Los Angeles decor. I repeated my environmental catechism: Yosemite was made a national park, and the Valley was saved for posterity; Hetch Hetchy was ruined for all time. It had a hollow ring.

In the spring of 1970 I returned to Hetch Hetchy, eager to repeat the serenely beautiful experience of the previous year. Joe Faint and Chris Jones joined me in an attempt to climb Hetch Hetchy Dome, a longer and smoother face than Wapama Rock. A full day of hard climbing gained us a huge

ledge below the unbroken, seven-hundred-foot final monolith. Above the ledge the unforgiving glacier-burnished armor plate of the dome was punctuated by only a single system of vertical cracks.

In the morning we awoke to find gray masses of vapor moving past us with great speed. Below, the view of the reservoir flickered as we built a fire and discussed the merits of continuing the climb. Soon, falling snow brought about a prompt decision, and I suggested that the best escape would be to traverse eastward into a large gully. Although it dropped away toward the reservoir in a series of overhanging steps, the gully's upper half appeared to reach the rim of the valley without any obstructions. From the rim we could travel cross-country for several miles until we hit a dirt road leading to the dam.

An hour later we had completed a touchy roped traverse off the ledge and were walking up the gully through thick brush in a heavy snowfall. Several inches of snow covered the ground by the time we reached the rim of the valley, and visibility was less than a hundred feet. After crossing a raging stream, we crashed for hours through deadfall in a trailless forest, trying to convince ourselves that although we had no idea where we were at the moment, we definitely were not lost. Navigating by the moss on cedar trees, we attempted to follow a course parallel to the rim of the valley. We soon reached a place where the horizon was suddenly darker, and the wind seemed to be coming from below instead of in front of us. I threw a rock and counted eight before it hit with a splash; at least we now knew the location of the reservoir. After an hour's more hiking we reached the roadhead, bedraggled and ready to embrace civilization.

Chris and I returned the following weekend, while Joe went climbing in Yosemite Valley instead. The intervening week had done nothing to lessen the difficulties of the lower section, and once again it took us a full day to reach the ledge at the end of the eleventh pitch. The fifth pitch is worth singling out. It followed a crack for a full one hundred fifty feet of con-

*Opposite page:
Joe Faint leading
direct-aid
climbing, Hetch
Hetchy Dome.*

sistent 5.8 and 5.9 climbing, with a 5.10 stretch at the finish. The lower half consists of a series of vertical lie-backs and hand-jams; the upper section is a continuous four-inch-wide crack, up which I wriggled with all the elegance of a dog chasing a cat through a storm drain.

Chris, who was not feeling well, relinquished the lead to me, and after what seemed like an eternity of exhausting direct-aid climbing, we finally reached the commodious ledge midway up the face. The spot offered so many amenities—room to stretch our legs, a natural spring, firewood—that our night could hardly be called a bivouac. We barbecued steaks over a roaring fire and bedded down on soft ground.

In the middle of the night I was awakened suddenly; something was tugging at the down jacket under my head. I turned on the flashlight and saw a ringtailed cat calmly eating my Juicy Fruit gum—wrapper, foil and all. Ringtails are supposed to be shy animals, yet this fellow sat munching on my rations with the gall of an alley cat. As we stared at each other, the light from my flashlight reflecting in his eyes, I wondered which one of us was the intruder. I could perceive no fear in his steady gaze but rather the calm assurance of a creature well in control of the situation. I began to resent his self-possession and looked around for something to throw at my uninvited guest. When I glanced back, he was gone into the night.

Before sunrise, Chris informed me that he felt much worse and might not be able to continue the climb. That he chose in the end to go on showed an extraordinary amount of determination. Although Chris is not a strong free-climber, he has a long record of major ascents in mountain ranges all over the world, demonstrating that more complex factors are involved in making big climbs than merely the technical ability to lead the hardest pitches. I felt a heavy weight on my shoulders that clear, calm morning. Climbing with someone who is ill is as difficult as solo climbing, but has the extra element of responsibility for another's welfare. I watched anxiously as Chris winced at the light from the sun as he followed a pendulum several leads above the ledge.

The climbing was mostly direct-aid in a single crack, which gradually dwindled into a water streak. Before it ran out, we reached a slanting horizontal ramp. With a bolt for protection, I face-climbed across the crackless ramp, feeling quite proud of my route-finding ability until I arrived at the end, where an unexpected blank headwall led to a marginal crack. By the end of the lead, I had placed two Bathooks, driven several shaky pitons, taken a short fall, skinned an elbow, and bruised an ego. Two bolts at the start of the next pitch gave me the confidence to free climb into a dihedral which led us to a ledge near the summit. Late in the afternoon we unroped at last and began walking up the inclined slabs to the crest of the dome. I felt happy and relieved; Chris was quiet and miserable. He was to spend the next week in bed recovering.

The walk back to our car provided a sharp contrast to our earlier retreat. Spring had arrived, and the greenness of life was everywhere. Only an occasional spot of snow in the shade of a log reminded us of the intense storm only a week before. Wildflowers carpeted clearings in the forest, and rivulets cascaded down every cliff. Hetch Hetchy had been trodden by people for more than a century, but on that afternoon we felt as though we had discovered it for the first time.

8
The
Moose's
Tooth

Talkeetna, Alaska.
Fifty-three residents, two airstrips, hundreds of dogs,
and two bush pilots who refused to speak to each other. At ten in the morning the main street looked like a
typical western town of the 1950s: two-lane road, dirt
shoulders, neon yet to come. Outside the town bar sat
two young men—one wearing Levi's, a sweatshirt,
and a crewcut; the other in a Hell's Angel-style leath-
er vest, cowboy hat, and gun belt. A wizened, almost-
blind Indian, leaning heavily on his cane, rattled the
door of the closed tavern. Age, alcohol, and twenty
hours of Alaskan daylight had fogged his awareness
of time. The bar did not open for many hours.

   Two young men carrying rifles walked in lock-
step in the main street, as a dusty Winnebago creaked
over chuckholes not ten feet away. The driver of the
Winnebago stared straight ahead at the pavement, ig-
noring the young men, who returned the compli-
ment. The motorhome rumbled on another hundred
yards to a dead end, where it turned around and
headed back and out of town without stopping.
Through the large, dusty windshield the motionless

Opposite page:
Yvon Chouinard
belaying on the
Moose's Tooth,
Alaska.

head of the driver seemed to form the pupil of a cyclopean, myopic eye, apparently unable to focus on anything but the road before it.

The true focus of the town was not the main street, however, but the dirt airstrip that led from the door of the tavern straight toward the river. A man dressed entirely in buckskin stood at the town end of the strip, negotiating with a pilot to airlift him with his dog team to a remote lake. He wanted a one-way fare; he had no plans for coming out. A prospector with tomorrow in his eyes approached me with a chunk of rusty metamorphic rock. "Gold," he said with evangelical emphasis. "It assays at over $200 a ton, but I've got to fly it out. I'd be rich if there was a road."

On the other side of the airstrip a chattering group of Japanese men wearing double boots and bright parkas busily crammed an enormous pile of equipment into a new Dodge van. In the distance, far beyond the town, beyond the river, and beyond the spruce forests, the Alaska Range loomed above the horizon. A forty-minute plane ride would soon transport us into an ice-age scene. As if traveling through a time warp, we would suddenly enter a Yosemite Valley of the Pleistocene, but one with a larger landscape and much higher rock walls, one where glaciers more than forty miles long plunged from alpine heights deep into wooded lowlands.

Our flight was delayed by a small oversight in logistics. Four of us—Jim McCarthy, Yvon Chouinard, Sandy Bill, and I—had come from different corners of the country to attempt the unclimbed 4500-foot granite face of the Moose's Tooth. Jim McCarthy had organized the expedition in New York. Since Yvon Chouinard owned a company that manufactured the best climbing hardware available, Jim had asked him to supply the expedition's pitons, carabiners, and chocks. Unfortunately, Jim's phone message failed to reach Yvon, so we met in Talkeetna with no equipment. It seemed that our climb might be over before it could start until Cliff Hudson, our bush pilot, located an expedition that had just returned from another

Opposite page:
Approaching the
4500-foot south
face of the
Moose's Tooth.

technical climb. When he asked if they would loan their gear to an expedition that included Chouinard himself, they looked at their Chouinard equipment and had a good laugh.

Jim McCarthy was the leader in our obstinate quest to climb an Alaskan big wall. Athough many snow and ice climbs of great difficulty had been made in the Alaska Range, none of its fabulous sheer cliffs had ever been climbed. A year earlier, in 1971, Jim had reached the 1800-foot level on the Moose's Tooth with Chris Bonington, Tom Frost, and Sandy Bill before a twenty-day storm drove the party back down. Only he and Sandy were returning. Sandy and Jim had also climbed together on the first ascent of the face of Lotus Flower Tower in Canada; they were well-matched for another go on the Moose's Tooth.

Chouinard, an incurable, grumbling romantic who had climbed a greater number of difficult alpine routes than any other American of his time, seemed at the moment to be going through a phase in which direct-aid climbing and long routes failed to hold his interest. While the rest of us discussed the Alaskan weather, Yvon kept talking about the surf in Southern California, but we hoped that once on the wall he would make the same remarkable effort that had gotten him up "impossible" faces all over the world. Yvon also gave us pause by asserting that a fast, light party could climb the Moose's Tooth in four days or less. Jim's idea of how to climb such a face was more conventional, and I concurred; I was terrified by the unknowns of Alaskan conditions. I wanted to bring hardhats, lot of wool, a fifteen-day supply of food, and waterproof hammocks. Chiefly, I wanted to stay alive at all costs.

The morning after the equipment impasse was settled we flew up the Buckskin Glacier toward the Tooth. The toe of the glacier was covered with debris, but as we moved from temperate zones into the arctic world, its surface became pure white, broken only by crevasses and an unexpected set of animal tracks that led tens of miles beyond the last timber. Cliff explained that they were wolverine tracks, but he could think of no reason why the animal would venture up the glacier—except that wolverines are obstinate creatures. He glanced at us and smiled.

The Cessna 185 landed in a glacial cul-de-sac directly underneath the great cliff. We set up a base-camp tent and spent the night listening to avalanches crash around us.

The walls blocked out most of the sky in all directions; we had the impression that we were looking up from inside a well. We feared that without a view of the horizon, predicting the weather would be impossible.

The very next morning we began the climb on wet, decomposing rock. Forty feet up the first pitch a huge piece of ice was plastered to the cliff as though an oversized, half-cooked pancake had been thrown against it. Beyond the ice patch, a single crack, aiming for the sky, split the monolith. We had climbed for twelve hours when it began to storm, and we set up our first bivouac on small ledges a thousand feet above the base. All of us used hammocks except Yvon, who decided to test his company's newest rain gear by bivouacking on a ledge less than a foot wide.

The rain stopped just after dawn. Jim, Sandy, and I assembled together on a ledge about fifty feet above Yvon, who expounded excessively on the fact that he had stayed totally dry. I began free-climbing an intricate traverse that Tom Frost had figured out the previous year. Jim, who was to follow, had contracted a mild case of dysentery from bad water in the Yukon. All night he had held back his bowels until they developed the urgency and capacity of a ready-mix truck caught in a traffic jam; as soon as I left the ledge, he defecated onto a tattered parka left behind by the previous year's party. When it came time to follow my lead, Jim tied the parka in a knot and threw it off the wall. This unlovely package opened in mid-air, raining its contents on the hapless Yvon, who instantly regretted his decision to spend the night below us.

As Jim started climbing, he began to feel worse. His face took on a cadaverous hue, and he vomited uncontrollably. I expected him to voice doubt over his

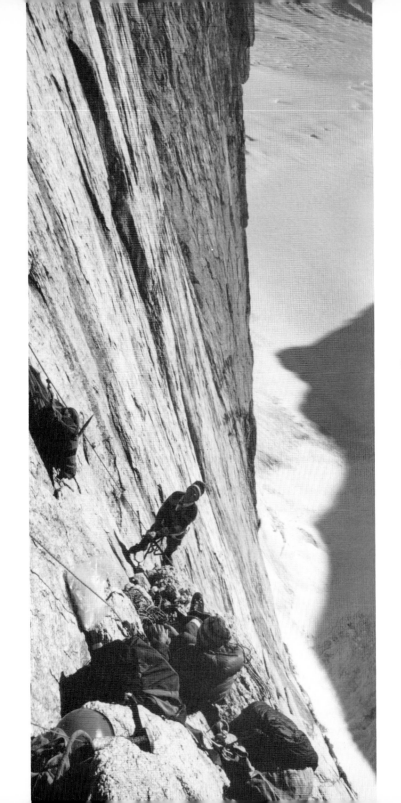

ability to make the final, unprotected traverse, but he said nothing; and I held my breath as he began a long, difficult diagoal up wet, rotten rock. He never faltered; his body had practiced hard face-climbing for so many years that he seemed to move by instinct. I never saw anyone move with such precision while feeling so poorly.

The quality of the rock continued to deteriorate as we climbed higher. On the first lead Yvon had used skyhooks on small flakes; by the fifteenth pitch I could remove any piton without a hammer and crumble the rock into gravel with my bare hands. Rockfall, too, became a serious problem. Missiles falling of their own accord from far above as well as rocks loosed by the leaders rained down on us. We all had brought hardhats except, as usual, Yvon, who claimed not to believe in them. After a particularly heavy barrage, however, he underwent a sudden religious conversion, and we began a ritual of reserving the three hardhats for the lower climbers. The unprotected leader was compelled to test his reflexes against the natural rockfall.

On the second evening we reached the first real bivouac spot on the wall, a sandy penthouse with accommodations for four. Although the ledge was wide, with enticing areas of level gravel that made perfect beds, that gravel could have come only from rockfall. If proof of the hazard were needed, two foam pads left behind during the previous attempt were almost completely covered by granite debris. I opted for another night in my hammock, in order to present as small a target as possible.

If our bivouac ledge was less than entirely safe, it had compensatory attractions. We were surrounded by bold beauty. In the distance was a perfect granite cirque capped with hanging ice. The monochromatic landscape of shades of gray was broken by a wreath of pink-and-green moss campion clinging to the face at the back of the ledge. It seemed magical that a single plant was able to survive in such harsh conditions. One pitch above the ledge we came upon a great hole in the granite; inside were fist-sized crystals of quartz,

Opposite page:
First bivouac on
the Moose's
Tooth.

Quartz crystals in a *vug*, mid-face on the Moose's Tooth.

tourmaline, and albite. We gathered a few loose ones and stuffed them into our packs.

In the morning Sandy and Yvon began leading above our high point. Jim waited on the ledge, still feeling under the weather but determined not to retreat. Sandy led a section of excellent rock; Then Yvon encountered the worst rock of the climb—so crumbling that he had to begin drilling exansion bolts next to a rotten crack that wouldn't hold pitons. I could sense Yvon's frustration. He had finally hit his alpine stride and was eager to complete the route, but the terrain wouldn't permit him to advance. We watched him rappel down without completing the lead and, shivering in an icy rain that had just begun, we held a council of war.

Sandy thought the route should be pushed and was against going down, saying that he'd climbed through worse conditions in the Alps. Jim wanted to descend because of his illness. Yvon wanted to descend because the rock was so poor that he could not recommend the climb to anyone; *ergo*, it was not worth pursuing. I was developing the same symptoms of nausea and diarrhea that Jim had. I was willing to stay if the majority went that way, but my heart was no longer in the climb. The issue was soon decided: we descended.

The twenty rappels down to the glacier lasted well into the night. When the ordeal finally was over, we gazed up at what we had thought would be the Mona Lisa of the alpine world. From this distance she looked beautiful, but we had touched her flesh and found gangrene. Since that attempt six years ago, several other parties have tried the east face of the Moose's Tooth; each one convinced, as we were, that the reality of the face must surpass the descriptions brought back by previous expeditions. None has even reached our old high point. Perhaps they learned their lesson more quickly than we did. I went back to try the face a second time in May 1973, hoping that clear weather and freezing conditions would make the route feasible, but one flight past the face revealed it to be dangerously plastered with snow and hopelessly out of condition. I led the expedition to within six hundred feet of the summit by a route from the opposite side, only to be stopped by an overhanging wall of rock even more rotten than that on the east face.

"Granite," according to a British encyclopedia of mountaineering, "varies from place to place but is always sound to climb upon and a great favourite with climbers." We had learned that all things in the wilderness are relative; a granite face does not always offer superb climbing, any more than skill and training guarantee success. In a larger sense, though, our failure on the Moose's Tooth only enhanced the mysterious attraction of the place, and it firmed my resolve to return to the great walls of the Alaska Range.

9
Free-
Climbing
Keeler Needle

IT WAS MY LEAD. I climbed thirty feet to the base of a smooth bulge where I stepped up and reached for a sloping handhold. My hand groped through loose gravel on the unseen shelf. Only ten feet separated me from easier going above, and I tried the same move again and again. No one had ever climbed those ten feet, and I realized then that neither would I.

I had been trying to bypass an overhang, and I was torn between two choices: relinquish the lead to Chris Vandiver, a better free climber than me, or attempt another way. I refused to consider a possible third choice: using direct aid placed in the rock to get past the difficult section. Why? Because three of us were attempting to free climb a rock face on Keeler Needle that had never been climbed without resorting to direct aid. It was just a game with us, but we were trying to play by the rules.

For decades the sport of rock climbing had been split into two factions: free climbers specialized in short, hard routes; big-wall climbers concentrated on long but technically easier routes. Wall climbs were

Opposite page: Keeler Needle (right) and Day Needle. The route on Keeler follows the prow.

81

traditionally approached with different equipment
and ethics than shorter free climbs. In the past, climbers recognized the stylistic purity of the short climbs
but considered free-climbing tactics impractical on
the long walls.

Was it possible to break these conventions? We
thought so. The overhanging east face of Washington
Column in Yosemite had already been climbed entirely free. The Diamond, a big wall on 14,225-foot
Longs Peak in Colorado, had also been free climbed
recently for the first time. Chris Vandiver and I had
done a free ascent of the west face of Mount Conness,
the sheerest wall in the High Sierra, only two months
before. After that ascent Chris had asked me if I
thought Keeler would also "go free." I wasn't sure,
having made the first winter ascent of the route with
heavy equipment and liberal use of direct aid. But
Chris's enthusiasm for the project proved infectious,
not only to me but to Gordon Wiltsie, the talented
High Sierra climber who in August 1976 became the
third member of our mini-expedition.

Just two weeks earlier we had retreated from the
same obstacle that was stopping us now: the tightest
spot on this section of the rock tower, a slightly lower
satellite of 14,496-foot Mount Whitney in the High
Sierra. I had tried a different way, an overhang normally climbed with pitons for direct aid. I thought at
the time about bypassing the overhang to the left, but
it was too late on a cold and windy day. My fingers
grew numb, the rock was rotten in critical places, and
I got scared. We descended and spent that night below the face, hoping for warm, clear weather in the
morning.

Dawn brought an incredible display of alpenglow,
turning Keeler Needle's granite to gold. Every crack
and rib was highlighted in bold relief. For several
minutes we watched in awe until the colors suddenly
disappeared. A hole in the clouds had closed, and the
landscape took on the dismal gray of the sky. Our
hopes for the climb wavered with the sunrise and
were extinguished completely when snowflakes began
to fall a few minutes later. We had no desire to at-

tempt difficult free climbing during a snowstorm.

All that morning, while our gear remained one hundred fifty feet up the face, we lay in our sleeping bags biding our time until the weather improved. Voices wafted out of the mist from the east face of Mount Whitney, the cliff next to the Needle. Two climbers we had passed on the trail were up there in the storm. Heavily laden with pitons, hard hats, down parkas, and bulky mountain boots, they could survive many days on the mountain if the need arose.

When the storm showed no sign of abating by noon, we decided to go home and return in better weather. Chris waited in camp while Gordon and I headed toward the Needle to retrieve our equipment. An hour later, as the two of us were descending with the gear, we talked about the nearby east face of Mount Whitney. Gordon said, "I'd like to climb it some day; I've never done it before."

"How about now?" I hinted.

"You're kidding!" he replied. "It's 2:30 in the afternoon, and it's snowing."

"No," I said. "I'm serious. If we climb unroped we can be up and down in just a few hours. We can handle the difficulties, even in this weather."

Just then we heard voices above: the other climbers were still on the route eight hours after they had started. Gordon looked worried, no doubt expecting to be benighted on the peak, but his adventurous spirit won out. "Okay," he assented, "Let's try it." Chris declined to join us because he had just climbed another route on the same face. As we began the climb, Gordon experienced mixed emotions; he enjoyed the freedom of climbing unencumbered, but missed the safety of the rope. Both of us compensated for the lack of security by increased alertness. We checked and rechecked potentially loose rocks and placed our fingers and toes with far more conscious care than when backed up by the umbilical cord of a rope.

Just below the summit we caught up with the other two climbers, who were outfitted like models in a mountaineering catalog. Seeing that we were unroped, they asked if we had climbed to the top of

Whitney by the horse trail and then had scrambled
down for a look over the sheer face. When we answered no, they asked where and when we had started
our climb. On learning that we had left the lake at the
base of the climb only an hour and forty minutes before, they expressed amazement at the speed of our
ascent. Actually, it was not so remarkable. The 1931
first-ascent party—four men wearing tennis shoes—
had climbed Whitney's east face in three hours and
fifteen minutes, unroped much of the way. Their
leader was Robert L. M. Underhill, a famous figure in
North American climbing history, who introduced
technical rock techniques to both the Grand Tetons
and the Sierra. In his account of that ascent Underhill
predicted, "I believe a good climbing party that knew
the route could ascend in something like half the time
we required." By this standard, our ascent was three
minutes slow.

Gordon was ecstatic when we reached the summit. We were able to relax; there was enough daylight
left for us to descend to the road before dark, and,
with no ropes or hardware to carry, the hike would be
pleasant rather than laborious. In many ways, our
spur-of-the-moment Whitney climb shared the same
spirit as our plans for Keeler Needle. Although we
would use ropes for safety on the Needle because of
the greater difficulties involved, we would avoid engi-
neering our way up the cliff. Our style would be more
akin to that of Sierra climbers of the Thirties than to
that of present-day big-wall climbers, and our accomplishment, if we succeeded, would mean more than
just an isolated "first free ascent." This effort was
part of a larger trend to merge the two disciplines of
wall climbing and free climbing. For years each specialty had gone its own way, but we believed that the
guiding principle of simplicity in mountaineering
must eventually bring them together again.

Two weeks after our Whitney romp, Chris, Gordon, and I were back on Keeler Needle for another
go. I climbed to the base of the overhang that had
scared me on the first attempt and found that nothing
had changed. The wall still swelled ominously over-

head, and the single crack was filled with loose rock. My attitude, however, was different: I knew that I could not climb the only alternate route. After carefully planning my intended moves, I climbed six feet toward the overhang and came back down; then I repeated the sequence, wanting to memorize this section so I could save my strength for the more difficult area above.

After a long rest, I yelled down to Chris, "Okay, I'm going for it!" He fed out the safety rope as I climbed upward. I expected each move to stop me—to force me to try a different technique, or worse, to prove so difficult that I would fall—but a minute later the crux was over, and I was resting in a wide crack before the final, easier moves at the lip of the overhang.

Most good rock climbers could have climbed the overhang as I did, without resorting to direct aid. The hardest move was barely 5.10, a rating near the top of the scale of difficulty but today commonplace in most rock-climbing areas. The main reason no one previously had free climbed that section of Keeler Needle was that no one had approached the route as an ordinary rock climb. The east face of Keeler Needle had always been considered a "big wall," a multiday climb requiring direct aid. Moreover, the face was an *alpine* wall where most climbers used gloves and stiff, heavy boots because of cold weather and snow.

Although we hadn't started until noon, we easily climbed more than half the face before dark. The absence of heavier equipment speeded our progress and enhanced the quality of the climb in countless subtle ways. I remembered one continuously difficult crack where I had used several direct-aid pitons in winter and watched with pleasure as Chris climbed the same pitch with hardly a break in motion. His thin shoes jammed perfectly in the narrow crack where earlier my mountain boots had grated on the outside edges. In spots where I had hung from pitons to rest, Chris stood comfortably with one foot jammed in the crack and the other on a tiny edge outside. He would climb ten or fifteen feet, pause to place a nut in the crack,

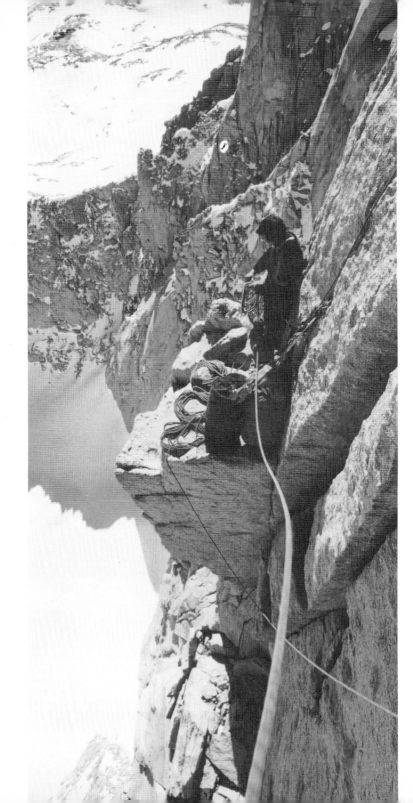

attach it to his rope with a carabiner for safety, then climb another section.

We reached a bivouac ledge at sunset and prepared for the night as we had each done many times before. We strung a rope across the ledge and attached it to several anchors in the rock; then each of us tied himself in. Darkness came quickly, but sleep eluded us for hours. We talked about climbs and friends we had in common; and when we tired of that, we gazed silently at the lights in the town of Lone Pine, fifteen air miles and 10,000 feet below our airy perch. We felt far removed from the world of hot sagebrush plains and civilization. Our own world was condensed into some nine hundred feet of granite, the distance between us and the summit.

In the cool, clear dawn, Chris, Gordon, and I sat huddled together, waiting for the sun's warmth to flow into us before we resumed climbing. After a cold breakfast, we packed all our gear into two medium-sized packs—quite a departure from most big-wall climbs where equipment must be laboriously hauled in huge bags up the wall. I felt almost guilty that the climb had required so little effort thus far. Spared both the drudgery of hauling heavy loads and the tedious work of hammering out long rows of direct-aid pitons, we were free to absorb the great beauty of Keeler Needle's setting. We were limited only by the extent of our skills rather than by logistical complexities.

Our test of those skills came very soon. I led an easy pitch to the base of a long corner. The next lead was Chris's, whose talent as a free climber is almost overshadowed by his exceptional control in tight situations. Because his movements are consistently smooth, many people who have seen him climb have found it impossible to tell where the real difficulties lie. I had climbed with him often and knew the telltale signs.

Chris climbed the first forty feet of the corner with long, fluid motions, stopping occasionally to place a nut in the crack for safety. Reaching a spot where the crack was about six inches wide and over-

Opposite page:
Tim Auger on an improbable ledge during the first winter ascent of Keeler Needle.

hanging, he found a row of expansion bolts on the wall next to the crack, marking where previous parties had ascended rope ladders clipped to the bolts. Chris wriggled halfway into the crack, which was too narrow for his chest and too wide for a fist- or knee-jam. At low elevations many climbers vigorously wriggle up such cracks, but to do so at 14,000 feet would almost certainly result in fatigue and a fall. Chris reduced his efforts to tiny movements that gained him only an inch at a time. His eyes brightened, and his expression grew intense as he used all his skill to keep from sliding out of the crack.

I watched him from the ledge below. Although his movements looked less spectacular than on many of the easier pitches we had already climbed, I knew that this impression was deceptive. Chris was making an incredible effort, but it was taking place inside—in the interaction of mind and body. Only he knew how closely he was approaching his limits.

Chris gained a large foothold and took a long rest; and when he resumed climbing, his movements once again were easy and graceful. Although the greatest difficulties were over, we weren't yet sure that the climb was in the bag. I couldn't remember every move from my last climb, but I did recall a long section of direct aid quite near the top. Throughout the rest of the morning the three of us alternated leads up the face, encountering only moderate difficulties. When we reached the place where I had used direct aid on my winter ascent, we saw an obvious bypass to the difficulties: a system of cracks that in winter had been plastered with snow and unusable. Now, however, Chris quickly traversed to the very prow of the Needle where an absurdly positioned ledge interrupted a curtain of granite that dropped in a single sweep. It looked like a window-washer's scaffold on the side of a skyscraper.

The difficulties were nearly over; even in winter we had free climbed most of the route above. The final pitches went quickly, and shortly after noon we reached the summit. It was, as always, a satisfying moment, but far more satisfying was the knowledge that we had accomplished our goal of climbing the big wall without big-wall techniques. We lingered only a few moments, then coiled our ropes, stuffed them into our packs, and descended a few hundred feet to a trail, where we merged unnoticed with the queue of weekend hikers heading for the summit of Mount Whitney.

From the summit we dropped down a gully into the mountain's afternoon shadow. Most shadows move as slowly as the hands of a clock, but Whitney's shadow chased us through the timberline paradise faster than we could scramble. It skimmed down cliff bands and boulders, slowing only for level sections of meadow and forest, until, like us, it traveled across the hot desert floor toward town.

10
Skiing the High Desert

THE GREAT BASIN extends from the crest of California's Sierra Nevada to the Rocky Mountains; it was so named by explorer John C. Frémont because it has no drainage to the sea. All waters in this vast region eventually run into alkaline "sinks" in the desert. Astronauts have reported that from outer space the Great Basin looks like a brown field sprinkled with giant caterpillars crawling south. The caterpillars are desert mountain ranges, more than fifty of which reach over 9000 feet in elevation. They are roughly parallel and separated from each other by flat, arid valleys. The view from the highest summits is a repeating sequence of distant ranges and valleys. It is like being in a giant room with mirrors on two facing walls: the images on both sides are similar and ever more distant.

Summer backpackers find these desert mountains hot, dry, and brown. Forests are sparse, lakes almost nonexistent, and fishing streams few and far between. Desert hikers usually head east or south of the Great Basin into the shaded, well-watered canyons of the Colorado River and its tributaries. In winter, how-

Opposite page: Bristlecone snag and Wheeler Peak (13,063 feet), near discovery site of world's oldest living thing, eastern Nevada.

91

ever, the Great Basin ranges become more like their alpine cousins. Their rounded crests become corniced ridges, and the sage blanket of the lower slopes disappears beneath snow. Temperatures often drop below zero; Jiggs, Nevada, below the Ruby Mountains, once recorded −55° F. The snow-covered desert ranges differ from the Rockies and the Sierra mainly in their long, open sections, exposed to the elements and unbroken by trees, cliffs, or shelter of any kind. It is this aspect that makes winter travel in the Great Basin a more serious undertaking than in the more alpine ranges of the United States.

After successfully traversing the crest of the White Mountains in 1974, I looked forward to another Great Basin ski adventure. A member of that trip, Dave Sharp, interested me in his home mountains, the Ruby Range, one of the largest in Nevada. Eventually, a total of eight people wanted to ski the 100-mile crest, so we split into two separate parties of four. We planned to meet in the mountains and travel together where feasible.

Early in the winter we skied up two side canyons and placed caches of food and fuel. Then we learned that Dave would be unable to join us for the final traverse. In his place we asked Mike Farrell, an experienced skier and climber, to join us. My group also included Doug Robinson, the first person to continuously ski the entire length of the John Muir Trail along the Sierra Crest, and Dave Lomba, a recent convert from the downhill slopes. George Miller organized the other foursome, which was composed of friends from eastern California.

In early March we returned to the Rubies and began skiing from Overland Pass at the south end of the range. On the first night we camped with George's group in the pinyon pine belt just above the open sagebrush at 6000 feet. For several days thereafter, we plodded through snowstorms. Forests became mystical places where somber forms suddenly materialized from the mist like headlights out of a fog, and the bristlecone pines seemed like pagan idols brooding over the inhabited valleys below. These contorted trees were fluted with rime ice that perfectly complemented their overall configuration—little wonder, since the same wind patterns that sculpted the ice had shaped the bristlecones over the course of thousands of years.

The previous winter, in another Great Basin range, Dave Lomba and I had tracked down the oldest living bristlecone ever discovered, a tree that had died in 1964—sacrificed to the cause of research. The story of its death had been hushed up; only by reading between the lines in scientific journals did it become apparent that a 4900-year-old tree with living branches had been felled and then sectioned with a chainsaw. At dawn on a March morning we found the tree's remains on a moraine at 10,750 feet below Wheeler Peak, the highest mountain wholly in Nevada.

Trees that have died natural deaths are often more beautiful than living ones, and I couldn't pass these ancient souls without being reminded of the words my mother had written when I was a child:

> The grandeur of Death in Nature! To see a tree that has lived and covered itself with foliage finally die, and for the first time show the Strength and Line of its limbs. To raise them naked and unashamed from the earth to the sky and there, silhouetted, to create for the whole world Beauty as it never before has been conceived.

I found death by the hand of man an entirely different matter. A stump protruded from a blanket of winter snow, and chunks of chainsawed wood lay in the snow like arms and legs on a battlefield. The Forest Service had granted geographer Donald Currey permission to cut down a tree in order to date Little Ice Age events. Currey used a special drill to remove a pencil-sized core from a tree more than 4000 years old. He missed the center of the tree, so he tried again. The tool broke off. Rather than wait months for a replacement, he asked that the tree be sawed into sections. In his scientific report Currey offers no

apology for the destruction of the earth's oldest
known living resident, which he fondly calls WPN-
114.

   After Currey's "discovery," the Forest Service invited a team of dendrochronologists to search for a
still older tree. But WPN-114 was an anomaly; no
bristlecone in that region was discovered within 1200
years of its age. Today the oldest living thing by de-

Remains of
#WPN-114,
Wheeler Peak.

fault is the Methuselah Tree in the White Mountains; its exact location is kept a secret for fear that tourists will desecrate it or carry off souvenirs.

Bristlecone rarely die in natural catastrophes. With the exception of an occasional lightning strike they grow too high and too far apart for fire to kill them. A few have toppled after gradual erosion of the mountain surface around them exposed their roots. Large trunks with bark on them lie at the bottoms of the steepest canyons in the White Mountains, apparent avalanche victims of the colossal winter of 1969. But the bristlecone's only real threat is from modern man; and in the twenty-odd years since humans "discovered" the tree, they have wreaked more damage than the previous 2000 years. The cool, clear wind that brightened Schulman's campfire in the 1950s now carries measurable air pollutants. Some of the oldest snags are gone, in the interest of science—and wood paneling. Others have found their way into campfires, wood stoves, and curio shops. Their very longevity makes them especially vulnerable to human impact. With growth rates often less than an inch in diameter per century, they cannot recover quickly from damage, as rabbits or eucalyptus can. Their survival—and ours as well—depends on slowing down the frantic scramble we call civilization.

In the Ruby Mountains we found bristlecones far more intact than those I had seen near roads in the White Mountains or near the sectioned tree on Wheeler Peak. Day after day in this harsh, untracked landscape we grew closer to the timeless world of the trees. One day of storm and drifting snow blended into the next. We forgot about sunlight. Our world was always gray and timeless. It was only winter, and there was only snow. Night arrived like a morning fog, softly and unannounced.

One morning a week into the trip, the storm was too heavy for traveling. By midday it abated, however, so all eight of us decided to ski down a bowl on the west side of Pearl Peak. It was a fantastic run: two to three feet of light powder lay on top of the many feet of settled snow. Unencumbered by our packs, we

floated silently down through open bristlecone forests, lost in the splendor of a white world with no firm
boundaries between earth, air, and sky. Here was wilderness skiing at its finest—superb conditions, as
good as the best of Alta or Aspen, in a paradise where
no one had ever skied before. I thoroughly tired myself by making six 1000-foot runs through the powder, each followed by an hour's climb back to the
crest.

The next day we looked forward to a descent of
nearly 3500 feet from the top of Pearl Peak, but the
view from the summit proved disappointing. The
slopes were extremely steep, and the avalanche danger was too acute for skiing. We chose instead to
climb down a long rock ridge, carrying our skis on
our packs. As we descended, the snow lost its fine
powder consistency, and minutes after we again put
on our skis, Dave Lomba's binding pulled out of his
ski, a mishap that had already occurred once before.
Taping it temporarily to the ski, we continued down
to an abandoned Basque sheepherder's cabin in an aspen grove by Smith Creek at 7000 feet to make more
permanent repairs. We fired up the old wood stove to
keep the room warm enough for the epoxy to set.

The next morning we were back on the trail, half
a day behind George's group. The canyon bottom was
serene, in sharp contrast to the harsh world of the
crest. Gone were the twisted pines, sandblasted by the
wind-driven snow and sculpted by a west wind that
was already blowing when men still lived in caves.
Here the trees were hardwoods—aspen and mahog-
any—and the sun-molded spring snow gleamed like
porcelain.

Two days later we climbed over the crest again in
rare clear weather. On the other side a steep glacial
cirque with open, high-angled slopes dropped to a
frozen lake. In the hour it took to reach the lake, the
weather had changed again. A storm seemed imminent. We found an old cabin built of roughly hewn
pine logs at the edge of the lake, and although it had
no windows and was totally dark with the door closed,
it seemed a more desirable shelter than our flapping

Opposite page:
Mike Farrell
skiing in the
Ruby Mountains,
Nevada.

tent, especially if the weather worsened during the night. Making it habitable proved to be more of a project than we anticipated, since it was filled nearly to the roof with snow. We spent hours digging it out, then chinked the holes in the roof and walls with blocks of snow and prepared for the night.

I awoke at midnight to the call of nature and ventured outside in sixty-mile-per-hour winds. The sky was cloudless, but the stars were dull, as though seen through a dusty window. By morning a real blizzard was in progress, and we quickly discovered how the cabin had filled with snow. Spindrift leaked rapidly through the timbers, covering us and all of our belongings. To add to our discomfort the temperature was well below zero; I spent the dark day inside my sleeping bag wearing all my clothes and my down parka. We wondered how far ahead the other foursome might be and where they were camped during the blizzard, but we needn't have worried—unbeknownst to us, they had given up on the tenth day of the trip.

I felt like a subject in a deprivation experiment. I'm the type that always has to be doing something, even if it's just scribbling or pacing the floor; but here there was absolutely nothing to do. For two days and three nights I couldn't read, write, or see the outside world. After two restless nights I realized how differently Doug Robinson experienced winter. He didn't think in terms of days of the week, hours of the day, or degrees of temperature. He was totally in tune with the wilderness of snow and sky: seeing without categorizing, traveling without scheduling, discovering without searching. He created another world for himself, one separate from ordinary reality. Only equipment tied him directly to the world he left behind.

Our stay in the cabin finally ended on the twelfth morning of the trip. It was windless, cold, and clear as we set off. Only ten minutes out, Dave ripped off his binding yet again. We spent an hour on a makeshift repair, hoping that we could continue along the crest for at least a few more days. But meanwhile the sky had clouded over, and strong winds created a ground blizzard. After a council of war, we decided to retreat.

The descent through a trailless, brushy canyon was an exhausting, all-day affair. Late in the afternoon we struck a dirt road and followed it to a modern ranchhouse. An old rancher came to the door and broke into loud guffaws of laughter; he had never seen anything like us before. Later we heard that his wife had spotted us walking up the road—colorful, muddy, and bedraggled—and when she had called her husband to the window, he had asked her in all seriousness, "Are them Indians?" We were treated to some gracious Western hospitality, and then the old rancher had his son drive us forty miles back to our car, where another surprise awaited us. The car had been burglarized of all our personal belongings, more than $1000 worth of everything from handmade equipment to underwear and tire chains. "Must have been those city people," said the rancher's son.

The sheriff's office was in a town nearly a hundred miles away. "Must have been some locals in the valley. Probably Indians," we were told there.

Although we had lost some of our most treasured possessions and had failed to travel the full crest of the Rubies, these misfortunes could not break the spell the high desert had cast. On the way home, we were already planning to traverse another lonely crest the following winter. As we drove west for hundreds of miles along Highway 50, snowy ranges rose before us. Here, so close to civilization, was an unofficial wilderness that remained virtually unexplored in winter.

11
A Vertical Mile in the Alaska Range

THE INTERIOR of the Alaska Range is an alpine world few people realize exists on earth: ice, rock, snow, and sky, each element in oceanic, overpowering quantities. Unlike the Himalayas, the landscape is nearly monochromatic. There are no greens, and yellows and reds appear only at sunrise or sunset. The scene is white, gray, and blue.

The giant rhythms of this land distort normal perceptions, and thoughts slow down like records played at too slow a speed. We humans have natural clocks, reset each day by sunrise and sunset, high noon and stars. But June in the Alaska Range has twenty-hour days followed by brief, starless twilights. Near the solstice, weather permitting, the sun shines all day on the summit ramparts of Mount McKinley, whose 20,320-foot bulk intercepts light beams aimed at the arctic circle nearly two hundred miles north. McKinley's shadow scribes a daily arc over thousands of miles of primeval landscape.

Well informed as we are about travel to the moon and planets, most of us know little of this ice-locked part of our own nation. In 1903 Frederick Cook fol-

Opposite page: Rime ice near summit of Mt. Dickey, North America's highest granite cliff.

The upper southeast face of Mt. Dickey

lowed the great shadow's arc around Mount McKinley in a 540-mile orbital expedition that has never been repeated. Three years later he was the first person to travel up the Ruth Glacier (named after his daughter) en route to an attempted ascent of McKinley. He discovered the Great Gorge, where some of the greatest granite faces in this hemisphere tower over either side of the glacier. True to the giant rhythms of the area, distances and features are much greater than they appear.

Until 1974 not one face in the Great Gorge had been climbed, and in the summer of that year I came to Alaska with Dave Roberts and Ed Ward to attempt the southeast face of Mount Dickey—the highest granite cliff in North America. The peak has a moderate snow and ice route up the back side, but drops a vertical mile to the Ruth Glacier and an unknown distance below the surface of the ice. The three of us had been on a combined total of more than twenty expeditions to the North, but our first sight of Dickey from the air still took our breath away.

As we were flown into the gorge by the legendary bush pilot Don Sheldon, days of foot travel were compressed into minutes of flight. Sheldon edged his supercharged Cessna 180 close to the wall for a look at our proposed route. Snow-covered ledges tiered like the windows of a high-rise building inspired both confidence, as resting places, and apprehension, as potential traps during a long storm. The areas has received more than eighty feet of snowfall in a single season. Much of the snow on those ledges had only recently been salt water in the Gulf of Alaska, perhaps lapping the sides of a Japanese fishing boat or roaring up Cook Inlet with the tide. Although we were now a stone's throw from the ledges, they were actually a hard week's work away.

We landed at Sheldon's "Mountain House," a tiny cabin he had built on a rock promontory on the Ruth Glacier to accommodate his clients. It was the only building for fifty miles around. At 2 a.m. the next moring we set off to climb Mount Dickey by the easy north side in order to cache a tent, food, and ice axes on the summit. At one point an invisible snow bridge collapsed, and I fell into a gaping hole. The rope snapped tight just as my skis struck a snow shelf inside the crevasse. Unhurt, I stared thirty feet overhead to the hole in the roof of the icy trap; by luck I had missed hitting hard ice nearby. Using mechanical ascenders, I escaped on a rope that Dave and Ed anchored above, and we continued the climb. The weather gradually enclosed us as we approached the summit ridge. We cached our supplies and descended by the same route to a col, marking our route with willow wands tagged with red ribbons. We camped on the col that night, then continued around the mountain to a base camp at the foot of the southeast face, where we waited through several days of poor weather to begin our ascent of the wall.

There was only on natural campsite on the vast glacier, a Shangri-la in the relentless, icy world. Base Camp was secure and friendly—warm clothes, level glacier, no bugs, no rockfall, no avalanche danger, plenty of food, and books to read. Boulders and gravel lay strewn on the ice, the beginnings of a lateral moraine. A flat, ten-foot rock was our kitchen, and a stream flowed into a deep blue pool nearby.

Our strategy was completely different than it had been on the Moose's Tooth two years before. Instead of bringing vast amounts of equipment and food in order to survive storms en route, we planned to go light and rush the face when a break in the weather came. To get a slight head start we spent a preliminary day fixing four ropes on the lower part of the face. The rock was firm, and the weather was as balmy as summer in the Tetons. Dave later wrote, "If we got no higher than this . . . we'd have had one great day of climbing, the like of which whole expeditions starve themselves for in the Alaska Range."

We planned to climb with only a three-day supply of rations—and no tent. We would have to move through the mountains' defenses for up to eighteen hours a day, quickly, decisively—a problem not unlike that of crossing a freeway on foot on a dark night. Better naked and fleet of foot than the deceptive safety of plodding caution.

After waiting out a short storm, we began the ascent beneath clearing skies on July 17 at 2 a.m. It was still early in the morning when we reached our previous high point at the top of the fixed ropes. The loads were the lightest I'd ever taken on a big climb, even back home in California. Relying on the snow, we carried little water. I had two wool sweaters and a rain parka—but no down jacket. We carried one tarp, one bivouac sack, one ice axe, and a single pair of

*Opposite page:
Dave Roberts
climbing on a
rare clear day in
the Alaska Range.*

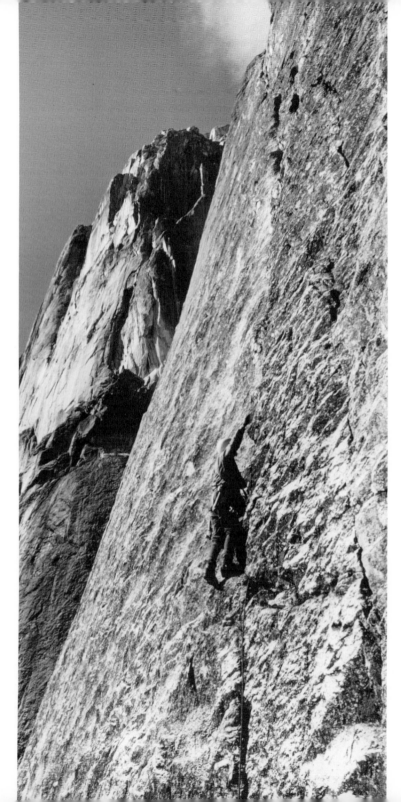

crampons—token gestures if conditions became extreme.

On the huge, complex cliff we felt like rats in a vertical maze. Each lead was a pathway which had to connect with the next in order for us to get through. Because we moved separately and concentrated intensely, our inward experiences were rarely shared. Dave would slow down on an unpredicted section of rotten rock, but neither Ed nor I would really ever know how bad it was. We'd see it as we mechanically ascended the rope after him.

"Nice lead, Dave."

"Thanks."

Then I'd watch Ed lead higher, back on firm rocks, moving confidently and using nuts and occasional pitons for safety. His hour of hard work, too, would rush by me in five minutes as I climbed the rope to take the lead above. Our progress was relatively rapid, about one hundred feet per hour. In other parts of the world this would work out to six nine-hour days of climbing to ascend the mile-high wall. Light gear, long days, and a little luck would put us on the summit in three days, in theory.

On the twentieth lead, about 2000 feet above the glacier, our mechanical ritual was halted by a series of problems. The rock was rotten and frostriven. A section of the wall that had appeared relatively gently angled now proved desperately dangerous. Higher, a vertical headwall of crumbly rock was broken only by a single flaw, a wide chimney hundreds of feet high. It was my lead, and using a rope traverse, I entered the chimney and found firm rock inside. Its sides were slick with water, however, and its few ledges covered by snow. My progress was blocked by giant chockstones, one of which required 5.9 climbing—close to the upper limit of difficulty on dry firm rock. The chockstone thrust outward like an awning, dripping water on my head. Jamming hands in the wet crack that connected it to the wall, I worked my way to the outside edge, reaching blindly over its brow into gravel and snow. A fall seemed certain so I backed down to a resting spot and then tried again, this time driv-

ing a piton into the crack near the lip. This would at
least protect me from a long fall, and I moved upward
more confidently, frictionig my boots against the flar-
ing walls of the chimney. They held, and I soon had a
death grip on a blocky handhold. At the end of the
lead I reached a ledge. The absolute clarity of my
mini-battle with the chockstone soon diffused into
dull anxiety about our progress.

Later that evening, Ed completed a diffcult pitch
in the ten-o'clock twilight, and we bivouacked on a
comfortable ledge. We cooked dinner and talked opti-
mistically about our progress: half the climb completed in a single day, with, of course, a head start of fixed
lines. Soon we were dozing beneath the clear sky.

The sunrise poured through slots in thick clouds
to spotlight summits with a strange orange phospho-
rescence. Yesterday we'd seen only occasional cirrus
clouds moving from the south like a giant migration
of geese, but today a storm was upon us. Valleys to the
south were locked in cloud, and streamers of white
mist crept up the Ruth Glacier, lapping at the base of
our mountain. In the gloom of four-o'clock dawn we
discussed whether to abandon the climb. Our decision to keep moving up was made out of psychological
commitment, not logic. There was a world of difference between the first and second day's climbing. The
vastness was suddenly gone, replaced by dank confine-
ment. Gone were the ice highways twisting through
distant gorges. The sky was depthless gray, as was the
air below our feet; clouds below me made the rope
disappear. At noon we reached an amphitheater surrounded by overhanging rotten walls and again found
the rock bad—so bad I could chop steps in it with my
alpine hammer. The only way out was to climb the
skyline to the right. Dave led to a ledge beneath a
steep headwall. On the next lead, he mistook my call
for "slack" to be a warning of "rock!" and instead of
feeding the rope, he pinned me for life's longest seconds on rotten rock high above a dubious safety anchor before he finally understood my yell. We had no
confidence that either pitons or nuts could safely anchor the rope in such poor rock. Imagine a floor cov-

ered with marbles. Make the pile of marbles bottomless, glue them together in some weak fashion, tilt the
angle to sixty degrees, and you have a rough approxi-
mation of the difficulties. Even in chopped steps my
feet felt insecure. It took me more than two hours to
climb a hundred feet up terrain that I knew I couldn't
climb down. Finally I reached a ledge—a triumph but
also a trap, for the cliff above was vertical and blank.

I had the dull feeling that we'd done something
irreversibly wrong, but Ed had a perpetual smile on
his face; I feared he didn't understand the gravity of
our situation. But Dave's notes on the climb contained a similar appraisal of me: "Would Galen
. . . keep that blithe cheerful countenance to the
end?" I began to understand why politicians smile.

Ed was still smiling as I lowered him around a
blind corner, to search out a route in the invisible
gloom. His voice, now more cheerful than his face,
warmed our hearts. "Perfect rock. It goes!"

Throughout the climb we could find no reason
why the rock was good in some places and bad in others. We knew that the bad rock was shattered by exposure to the elements, but the good rock was the
same quartz monzonite and good and bad were often
found side by side on similar exposures. The good
rock was climbable even when it was overhanging; the
bad rock was virtually impossible as it approached the
vertical.

We were lucky to have escaped the amphitheater
before the storm began. A few hours' delay and the
rock would have been plastered with snow. We
climbed all afternoon on fine rock, wondering when
the storm would begin and hoping that its slowness
was not an indication of its size. By early evening it
had begun raining, and we stopped on a giant ledge
about 1000 feet below the summit.

The rain turned to snow, and a strong wind came
up. An Alaskan blizzard was upon us. Dave covered
himself with the tarp and slept in a small nook; Ed
crawled into the bivouac sack and remained exposed
on the ledge. Blanketed with snow and curled in fetal
position, he looked, Dave said, "like a victim's body

discovered by rescuers." I wriggled into a natural coffin under a boulder. Protected from the wind, but exposed to blowing snow, I spent the night so cramped that had the rock shifted half an inch I would not have gotten out. Sleep came slowly, and my thoughts drifted.

If we were successful, would our climb be considered just another gymnastic feat? Would failure, whether by a hairbreadth or a calamity, make us look foolish to have even attempted the climb? We asked no rescue, and none was expected. How different our situation might be if, as in Switzerland, a téléphérique went up Mount Dickey and a rescue crew was even now lowering a cable. How many men, how many planes, how many changes would it take to destroy our remote experience in this alpine sanctuary?

Mount Dickey, unlike most of the McKinley massif, was not in a national park. It was currently unprotected but was included in a large southern extension proposed for Mount McKinley (now Denali) National Park. On an earlier expedition I had seen no threat of development to the lands that constituted the southern extension, and I doubted the need for official protection. I suspected that the minimal development that always comes in a national park's wake might be more damaging to the region than leaving it alone.

I've since changed my mind; I had drawn a romantic comparision between this land and Yosemite National Park. I had seen the Ruth Gorge as Yosemite had been in the Pleistocene epoch. Its ice hasn't melted, most of its peaks are unnamed, and it is rarely visited. In sharp contrast are the stores, golf course, jail, and bank of Yosemite proper. A national park in this part of Alaska had seemed grossly premature, but it now seems obvious that development throughout post-pipeline Alaska is imminent. The time for parkland is now. (In December 1978 the proposed extension was made into Denali National Monument.)

The existing Denali National Park is not plagued by the excess development so common in parks of the lower forty-eight. Its harsh climate and remoteness protect it, but a large share of the credit must go to its early superintendents. Three of the first four were men who had climbed Mount McKinley. Unlike most modern park managers, who acquire their jobs by administrative musical chairs, they had a hard-won, intimate appreciation for the land. Today most important park decisions come from Washington, but Harry Karstens, Denali's first superintendent, was in a unique position. Not only had he led the first ascent of Mount McKinley, but he had also shared in the very birth of the idea of making a national park when he wintered north of the mountain with naturalist Charles Sheldon a decade before the park was created.

If John Muir could see Yosemite today, he would certainly question the idea of national parks. Denali National Park, however, is a monument to the national park idea and the goals of Sheldon and Karstens as they sat around campfires in the mountain's great shadow. The only indoor accommodations are at the park boundary. Fewer than one hundred campsites—and no other accommodations—exist along the eighty-seven-mile dirt road that crosses the park. Except for those with campsite registrations, all visitors must ride tour buses or walk through the park; pri-

Canada lynx at Teklanika River, north of Mt. McKinley.

vate vehicles are banned. In contrast to the lifeless ice and rock of the Ruth Gorge, the park road traverses green, rolling tundra and spuce forests. Control of mechanized transportation keeps North America's finest wildlife viewing area much the way Sheldon saw it in 1906. During a single day in the park I saw moose, caribou, eagle, gyrfalcon, ptarmigan, porcupine, beaver, grizzly, Dall sheep, wolf, and, most remarkable of all, a lynx stalking a snowshoe hare forty feet away from me. To have this—and the Great Gorge—in a single national park would give Denali the finest cross section of wilderness in any park in the world.

The morning after our bivouac in the storm, I peered out at a white world from high on Mount Dickey. A blizzard filled the air with snow, and rime ice clung to the rock above. It looked like photographs I'd seen of the north face of the Eiger in storm. I was wet but warm in my fiberfill bag, and I suggested that we try to wait out the storm where we were. Both Dave and Ed wanted to head for the summit. I was worried about technical climbing with icy ropes, but descending 4000 feet in a storm was out of the question, and we had no inkling of how long it would last. Conditions could get much worse before they got better. Because we were running low on food, we agreed to continue climbing.

Using our only crampons and ice axe, Dave took the lead, and we soon came to a sudden juncture with dark, stratified, metamorphic rock held in place by ice and snow. Above, the angle of the face averaged sixty degrees, and the surface was about half rock and half snow, although much of what looked like snow turned out to be ice. We regretted not having more ice axes and crampons but, on the other hand, they might have slowed us down on the two previous days of rock climbing.

How totally different from our beginning on dry rock and a sunny day! It was as though we had switched to a different mountain on a different continent. We climbed roped together in a claustrophobic world of blowing snow, with visibility often less than one hundred feet. Our rate of progress slowed to a vertical crawl. Even Ed dropped his ever-present smile to say, "I don't like this. It seems real dangerous."

Dave, on the other hand, exuded confidence as his clawed feet led the way over icy black rock. He smiled and made quick decisions, seemingly totally in control of the situation. He was carrying a detailed photo of the face, now crumpled like a handkerchief, and occasionally he stopped to correlate features. As we moved higher we found progressively less rock and more snow, and finally we came to a place where everything above was white. Dave announced that we were close to the top. Estimating the angle would ease off in fifty feet or so, he climbed directly up steep ice and soon became a dark shadow in the snowy tempest. After climbing one hundred fifty feet without seeing an end to the ice, he retreated.

Ice from Dave's footsteps crashed down on our hardhats. Our smiles had entirely vanished by now; we were cold and disillusioned in the blowing storm, perhaps even lost. We began traversing hundreds of feet to the south, searching for a weakness in the continuous ice wall. We wanted rock outcrops for belays and piton protection, but rock was the exception and snow the rule. Our diagonal traverse angled upward, and Dave occasionally stopped to belay us individually over steep sections. I slogged through deep snow and climbed over a small cornice onto unexpected level ground. Dave shook hands with me, saying he thought we were on top. But where? We were in a white-out.

Ed soon joined us. At first we didn't agree on which direction to head on the broad summit plateau, but we decided to walk blindly south. Suddenly, through the storm, a tall flagpole appeared with a large, red flag blowing in the wind. I stared at it in disbelief: Who could have put such a thing near the summit of Mount Dickey? It hadn't been there a week before. We must not be in the right place. It took only a few seconds for these thoughts to race through my mind, and as I took another step, my error perspective became obvious. it was one of our four-foot-tall willow wands with a small red ribbon, glowing from the shadowless murk of a white-out.

As we continued across the plateau, new wands appeared like tail lights out of fog until we came to our tiny cache. Two ice axes for the descent; one two-man tent, crowded for three, but luxurious compared with our previous nights' accommodations; and two days worth of freeze-dried food. These meager things were a pot of gold, and we were soon resting in the tent, tired, cold, satisfied.

Climbing into a storm high on Mt. Dickey. Moose's Tooth is in background.

12
The
Cirque
of the
Unclimbables

IN THE SUMMER of 1972, my friend Jim McCarthy and I flew in his small plane toward Jim's favorite spot on earth—the Cirque of the Unclimbables, an isolated group of granite peaks in the Logan Mountains of Canada's Northwest Territories. Located in a completely roadless area larger than California, the cirque is so remote that at the time of our visit fewer than twenty-five people had ever set foot there, although it is more spectacularly beautiful than any place I have seen in the national parks of North America.

Jim and I had just returned from an unsuccessful attempt on the Moose's Tooth in Alaska, and he assured me that the Logan Mountains, although at the same latitude, had far better weather than the Alaska Range. He had first visited the area a few years earlier, making the first ascent of Lotus Flower Tower in several warm, twenty-hour days. After a wretched spell of Alaskan rain and snow, we were ready for such a sunny paradise.

Our flight in Jim's Cessna over the vast, unpopulated reaches of the North provided a classic contrast

Opposite page: Meadow under Mt. Harrison Smith, Cirque of the Unclimbables, Canada.

115

between timeless nature and timebound man. The little plane was fully equipped for instrument flying. Often we slipped into the translucent void of a cloud bank, and I would watch Jim scan the panel and recreate in his mind the dynamic perspective of his craft moving across the landscape. Gradually I began to realize the limits of the various devices. When a call to an airport gave us a new barometer reading, Jim dialed it into the altimeter. The needle moved up. The plane did not. It was theoretically possible to read 2000 feet of ground clearance on a gauge a split second before slamming into the side of a mountain. The magnetic compass wigged and wagged as we passed near ore bodies. Nothing was absolute, I thought to myself, except time. Every thirty-six seconds, a new digit snapped into the hundredth's place on the gauge that registered hours.

But how absolute is the human conception of time? As we flew north across Canada, the dwindling number of settlements below us made it seem as if we were returning to a time long past in the United States. Calgary, a potential Canadian Los Angeles, quickly sprawled into a checkerboard of farms. The fields were dotted with small patches of forest, the only remnants of what was once an unbroken expanse of woodlands and lakes. Gradually the farms grew fewer until they became islands in a sea of lakes and forest, and in the Yukon, signs of man became still less frequent. Regardless of the regular ratcheting of the hour gauge, we were traveling backward, not forward, in time.

We landed the plane on the dirt airstrip of a small mining town. On a hillside above a long valley was the open pit. Ten-ton Euclid trucks howled back and forth on the Z-shaped road from the pit to the groaning and clanking processing mill in town. Pipes gushed black water into siltation ponds. Abandoned cars, empty oil drums, bits of lumber, and sewage formed a wreath around the town; tungsten and people were the only things carried out. A portly woman in her forties came riding down the hill on a motorcycle. We met her later in the mess hall and learned that she was the cook for the single men living in the dormitories. She offered us food and coffee, and I commented on both the quality and quanitity. "The boys get lots of good food and high pay," she replied. "They have to. A person needs that and more up here or else he'll go crazy. In the winter it sometimes goes seventy below, and the days are only for hours long. Most everyone has snowmobiles. In the summer people play baseball, go hiking, swimming—I ride a motorcycle, you know. A person has to have something else besides working. Why one fellow, he worked lots of overtime and did nothing but work, eat, and sleep. We warned him, but he wouldn't listen. They carried him out of here in a strait jacket."

An hour later we were in a jet helicopter, crossing icefields and snowy ridges on our way to the heart of the mountain range. Blue lakes lay below peaks in glacier-carved bowls. Far below the hanging alpine valley were the trenches of the main rivers. The long hours of summer sun had melted the surface of the permafrost, changing level valley floors into impassable brush-tangled bogs that formed moats around the granite cathedrals in the center of the range.

The helicopter deposited us and our pile of gear in an alpine meadow and flew off. We planned a multi-day ascent of nearby Parrot Beak Peak and brought food for five days; the helicopter was to return on the fifth. Granite towers thousands of feet high loomed over the small meadow where we pitched our tent.

That evening I took a long walk into the next valley. From the air the vegetation had appeared uniformly green, but on closer inspection, the verdant grasses and mosses proved to be merely the dominant color in a melange of hues. The north sides of the rocks were splotched with colorful lichens; the south sides carpeted with thick mats of yellow moss. Streams were gray, not blue, because they were laden with glacial silt. Wildflowers grew in profusion on the meadowed benches. Rivulets snaked through the meadows and dipped off into the distance. I felt like an intruder as my footsteps squashed down the living mat.

I walked through a meadow decorated with tremendous squared boulders. One gigantic rock was split in three parts and through a narrow crack I could watch clouds swirling around the tops of towers. It gave me the unmistakable impression of being in a natural Stonehenge. Timberline was at only 4000 feet, and this meadow was far above the last trees. I saw marmots, finches, ptarmigans, and plenty of signs of mountain goats. I was surprised to find a dwarfed spruce growing behind a boulder in less than two inches of caribou moss. Although it had more than twenty sets of limbs, it was no more than eight inches tall. I would have taken for granted the most stately spruce, but this lone, small tree caught my attention and made me wonder how long it could last. Morning dawned gray and cloudy. Jim and I agreed to delay our multi-day ascent and instead chose to climb a shorter but fine-looking buttress on the highest peak in the region, Mount Sir James McBrien. After three hours of unroped scrambling, we reached the beginning of technical climbing. A few hundred feet higher we came to a steep headwall. It was my turn to lead. Climbing here required a more cautious attitude than in a more accessible region; in case of injury or sickness, one might wait a long time to be evacuated. My feet began to twitch involuntarily, and I placed three pitons within arm's reach to protect one move over a difficult 5.10 ceiling.

Reaching the summit early in the evening, we saw a storm advancing from the other side of the peak. The complex descent on the easiest side of the peak involved traversing narrow ledges and kicking steps down snow-filled couloirs. Lower down we found fresh goat tracks and followed them onto a well-worn trail across grassy ledges. As we rounded a corner, I spotted a family of five goats ascending a nearby ridge. It was ten o'clock that night before we reached our tent in the rain.

It was still raining the next morning, and it continued for three more days without stopping. Around noon on the third day, Jim discovered that our beautiful meadow was fast becoming a lake. Although we had chosen the highest piece of ground, it was only six inches above the overall level; the water was rising fast and we were already on an island. Within five minutes we were furiously digging trenches with ice axes, defending our little portable environment against an onslaught of silt-laden water—the same waters which had created the meadow from a trap basin in the glacial moraine. It didn't work; the water was coming from every direction, faster than we could drain it with our crude tools. We paused to take stock of the situation and then spotted the main source of the water—a large stream puring down the hillside just above the meadow. We concentrated our efforts there, building dams and trenching until we had altered the course of the stream to avoid the meadow completely.

Jim McCarthy celebrating "victory" over nature.

It would be nice to be able to say that we considered all the alternatives and chose one that was both practical and environmentally sound. However, I can't recall either of us suggesting that we simply move up onto the rocks and huddle under a tarp. How ironic that we who talked of preserving this place were busy trenching and damming at the first threat of getting wet. We even felt proud of our efforts. I finally understood how Floyd Dominy must have felt when he dedicated Glen Canyon Dam. All the same, I was horrified at my thoughts. Just a week earlier, flying over endless miles of woodland, I had experienced similar feelings when I found myself thinking, "Why are they cutting all that beautiful timber in California when they could be logging up here and nobody would miss it?" I quenched the thought immediately but recognized that for a moment I had experienced the frontier ethic of the North.

There was nothing to do now but wait in the tent. I teased Jim about his weather prophecy. He said the rain would quit soon, but I noticed him toying with his dismantled survival rifle and began to consider the serious possibility that we might be trapped here long enough to need it. When we awoke the next morning it was snowing. The clouds parted for a brief glimpse of the cliffs, and the scene was wild beyond description. Towers plastered in white loomed somberly out of the mist. A foot of snow lay on our meadow, and the goat paths on the mossy ledges were buried. Falling snowflakes dampened the acoustics of the cirque; except for the roar of an occasional avalanche, all was still.

The sixth day passed. Our food supply was very low, and we talked about what we could do if the helicopter never came. It might take us weeks to hike the fifty miles of brush and marshes between our cirque and the mine town. Suddenly I was no longer in a comfortable living room thumbing through a picture book of wilderness images. Here, in trouble, the value of civilization came clear. The embarrassing pride we felt over damming the stream, my flash of faulty logic about logging the North, and our present helplessness all began to fit together. I needed the tools of civilization. What did I have that I could do without? My mountain boots? My food? My sleeping bag? Without the umbilical cord to civilization that these things represented, I would be in bad shape. Back home, I had been lulled into false confidence in my own survival abilities by the nearness of civilization. I could reach habitation in two days of hiking from the most remote area in California.

In strict terms, much of what passes for a "wilderness experience" is counterfeit. Once in a while someone really does make a break for a short time— often it is accidental, termed "exposure," and results in a visit to a hospital. The "ruggedness' of a wilderness experience is not merely the physical effort involved, but the chance that the conditions of nature will exceed the capabilities of the equipment we bring with us. In other words, we risk being thrown into a true wilderness situation, one that modern people carefully avoid by special equipment, clothing, and rations.

Jim and I had brought an element of the technological world into the backcountry. Mountain tents do considerably less damage than many other kinds of portable environments, such as recreational vehicles, but even the most adaptable selfcontained travelers, wilderness backpackers, leave their marks. Footsteps gradually wear footpaths; campfires gradually develop into permanent campsites, and the pursuit of the unknown sooner or later becomes a section in a guidebook. Even though backpackers are equipped to deal with a far wider set of circumstances than are recreational vehicles, when the limits of their adaptability are exceeded they must either suffer or change the land to suit their needs, as we had chosen to do by trenching and damming.

In the natural world, an animal must adapt to its environment or perish. Civilization implies adapting the environment of human needs; much of the appeal of wilderness is that it can return people to the primeval situation to which humans are adapted. Keeping equipment down to a few simple items is one step to-

ward this goal, but many people become more concerned with the means than the ends. Equipment is counted and compared like batting averages. The differences between various brands of equipment are far down the list of things that the modern, urban person needs to know in order to understand and enjoy the wilderness.

I peered outside the tent into a mist-shrouded dreamland of meadows, streams and granite towers. A heavy rain was washing the snow from the meadow, but it was still snowing on the summits. The scene was magnificent, but I longed to be back in the mining town, though a week earlier I had scoffed at its prefabs, snowmobiles, and life styles. Once again the ethic of the North had caught up with me; it is hard to consider the intrinsic value of wilderness while it is a real adversary. In the United States, we are beginning to realize that our wildlands are finite, but in the Northwest Territories, an earlier spirit prevails. The people of the North are not wrong, any more than Americans were wrong to drive cars without smog devices in 1935, or to shoot buffalo when there were millions of them. Modern pioneers are living in a different age. Their daydreams are still of the future, and their frontier heroes have modern equipment. Today's Abraham Lincoln lives in a log cabin with central heatng and a freezer full of moose. Today's Snowshoe Thompson has treads and makes rather more noise. And today's Davy Crockett—I met him in person, in Alaska—dynamites coyotes from his airplane. "Thirty-dollar bounty and you get to keep the pelt, you know."

My mental ramblings might not solve the problems of the developing North; but I did gain an increased awareness of how thoroughly we are trapped in our own time—I in mine, and the pioneers of this land in theirs. They must live through the same mistakes made by earlier pioneers before they can realize what they have lost. As for me, I still had to think in terms of basic survival. There was a helicopter buzzing in the back of my consciousness, and I hoped it would soon appear in reality.

Opposite page:
Tent near Lotus
Flower Tower
and Parrot Beak
Peak.

The eighth morning dawned gray. Rain was intermittent, and fog hung low in the distant river valleys. Clouds still veiled the summits of the peaks. I put on my wet boots and stepped outside. Every watercourse was full. I grabbed my pack and a camera and announced that I was going for a walk. I'd gone only a hundred yards when the humming of the water was drowned out by a gradually increasing noise; I barely beat the helicopter to the tent. Suddenly time was of the highest value. Minutes ticked by at hundreds of dollars per hour as the helicopter waited for us to dismantle our camp. Darting around the meadow, we must have resembled the frantic, choppy characters in an early silent film. The pilot seemed puzzled that we took the time to bag up garbage and tie it into the baskets.

As we rose into the air, we had a view of the lower meadow completely submerged in water. We were witnessing the forces of its creation still at work today. But the silt-laden water was prevented by our earthworks from reaching the meadow where we had camped. We had been thoroughly conditioned to pick up garbage, even at great cost; but we had not thought of tearing down the dams during our expensive rush to return to civilization. Unconsciously, we had placed a dollar value on nature's chosen course for a mountain stream. I looked back at the sheer 2000-foot face of Proboscis, as impressive as Yosemite's Half Dome, following the clean granite with my eyes until it abruptly merged with jumbled red rock. A contact-metamorphic zone: what every prospector seeks when hunting copper, lead, and gold. The list could continue—tungsten, molybdenum, silver, zinc—but the meaning was the same. Call it progress, manifest destiny, the ethic of the North—time could all too easily catch up to these mountains.

When I returned home I wrote about our visit without using a single place name. I wanted to emphasize the nature of the experience rather than the place itself, and I feared that the area might be damaged by overuse if my article attracted too many visitors. Through word of mouth and mountaineering journals, the Cirque has since become well known to climbers all over the world, and the experience is no longer the same. There is garbage in the meadows and the solitude is gone. What I choose to remember is the feeling of moving backward through time, back to the kind of experience enjoyed by the early explorers of the Grand Canyon, of Yellowstone, the Grand Tetons, or Yosemite; back to the time before these scenic wonders became islands of wild country surrounded by cities, roads, and farms. Finding this experience in North America in the 1970s was the journey's greatest reward.

13
Around
Mt. McKinley
on Skis

IN 1906 THE EXPLORER Frederick Cook reported that his fast, light expedition had made the first ascent of Mount McKinley in only eight days. Cook's climb was soon discredited, however, and the rest of his life unfolded as if the hoax had been branded on his forehead. His claim to have reached the North Pole in 1909 was disbelieved mainly on the basis of the Mount McKinley episode, while Admiral Peary's polar jaunt, reported to the world at the same time and with even less documentation, was accepted as authentic. (The consensus of present-day authorities is that neither explorer actually reached the Pole, although both spent considerable time very far north.) McKinley figured yet again in Cook's life, when the climbing hoax was mentioned in a judge's verdict convicting him of selling useless land in Wyoming as oil property during the Teapot Dome scandal. Cook spent more than a decade in federal prison; his confiscated lands, in which his life savings had been invested, eventually produced more oil than he had ever promised prospective buyers. On his deathbed, he was pardoned by FDR.

Opposite page: Doug Weins jumping a crevasse at the head of the Peters Glacier near Mt. McKinley.

127

Like other explorers, Cook named many of his geographical discoveries, but his names for the most part have disappeared from modern maps, and his actual achievements are all but forgotten. One of his more unusual adventures was a land circumnavigation of Mount McKinley in 1903. Up to that time, the approaches to the highest point in North America were unknown, and Cook spent four months making a 540-mile orbit along rivers, through forests, across passes and glaciers. For three-quarters of a century to come, no one else circled the mountain on the ground.

When I circled McKinley in a small plane in 1972, I was amazed by the interconnecting pattern of five major glaciers, each one longer than any in the Nepal Himalaya. They flow down the peak's flanks and abruptly turn to form a ring of ice ninety miles in circumference and shaped like the outline of a cotton-wood leaf. McKinley's great circle of moving ice, entirely above timberline, is unique among the 20,000-foot peaks of the world. The great circle would have become a popular ski-mountaineering route years ago were it not for one problem: the mountain's three major buttresses trisect the route at elevations of 10,000 to 12,000 feet. This makes the difficulties involved in circling the mountain even greater than those of climbing it. In the last two decades, several groups attempted the circle, but were forced to retreat by frostbite or technical difficulties. My own eagerness to ski such a great natural route was tempered by the realization that packs might weigh 100 pounds, a broken ski could be devastating, and certain icefalls might prove impassable.

In 1978 I was invited to join the Mount McKinley Great Circle Expedition. Ned Gillette, an Olympic cross-country skier in 1968, had full financing from some Norwegian ski companies to attempt an "orbit" far tighter than Cook's. It would be the first within the limits of the peak's glacial systems and would follow the precise route I had studied from the air. Had the choice been mine, I would have brought sturdy downhill skis with mountaineering bindings, but Ned wanted to prove the strength of the light touring skis and narrow, fifty-millimeter racing binding that he used on packed tracks. He had already used "skinny skis" to cross Ellesmere Island, the land mass nearest the North Pole. Our foursome consisted of Ned and myself plus Alan Bard and Doug Weins, who had skied Ellesmere in 1977. All of us had the climbing experience necessary to cross the three icy ridges that separate the glaciers.

We estimated that the Great Circle would take about three weeks and require two food caches. On April 7 bush pilot Cliff Hudson landed us on the Kahiltna Glacier, just outside the boundary of Mount McKinley (now Denali) National Park. Each of us was in shape for cross-country skiing and for carrying big loads—our packs weighed ninety pounds—but not for both together. We skied off with all the grace of newborn calves, and instead of linked figure eights, our tracks down the first easy slope resembled a child's by-the-numbers sketch, each circled number corresponding to a crater in the snow.

Three days and one storm later, we reached our first obstacle, Kahiltna Pass on the West Buttress. It was −12° F as we started up what appeared to be a forty-degree snowslope; we quickly discovered that a thin frost layer lightly covered blue ice underneath. I led a full rope length on front points without finding a belay. With our second and last rope tied on, I reached a snow-covered crevasse about two feet wide. I couldn't place a secure screw in the rotten ice, and my axe sank too easily into the powdery snow outside the crevasse. I dug my way inside and sat on a snowbridge directly over the rope; if the screw and axe pulled out, I planned to become a human anchor by jumping in.

When we reached the crest of the Alaska Range, we could see beyond peaks coated in a winter armor of blue ice toward endless white plains to the north. Below us, the Peters Glacier stretched smoothly into the distance. To gain the head of the glacier, we descended several thousand feet of steep snow. The surface of the glacier was a frozen ocean of icy waves and swells; a ground blizzard driven by high winds added a mystical haze to the landscape.

We found little time to contemplate the great beauty of the scene, however, for without metal ski edges, we fell down repeatedly. Alan took an especially bad header and dislocated his shoulder. He stood up in pain, popped the joint back in with his own tug, and held his arm helplessly against his chest. We set up camp immediately, wondering if two of us would have to make at least a week's journey out to summon a rescue.

In the morning Alan was able to continue, but on foot instead of on skis. Luckily we were now on a section of hard windslab rather than the powder snow of earlier days. That afternoon Alan decided to try skiing, timidly on gentle slopes. He was afraid of losing control on the downhill runs, but the conditions made this impossible. The surface of the entire lower glacier was underlain with depth hoar—bottomless sugar snow formed in cold, dry conditions—and for the next two days we were held to a pace of two miles in ten hours. Typically, we alternated from knee-deep snow to sudden holes of thigh-deep crystals that rolled underfoot like ball bearings. This resulted in frequent falls, always onto one's back, followed by the tiring struggle to get up again. I was reminded of a cartoon that showed a backpacker lying on his back by a trail, his arms and legs flailing, and one observer commenting to another: "I hear they die if you don't turn them over."

From the wretched Peters Glacier, we headed up Gunsight Pass and onto the Muldrow Glacier. The depth hoar was gone, and we had easy sailing for several days as we turned up the Traleika Glacier toward the East Buttress of McKinley. We were through the easy half of our circle, and by this time our individual roles in the expedition had become clear. Ned was our leader. His job was to make decisions when there was a difference of opinion on how to proceed, but we always wanted to do the same things; so instead he busied himself with watching his carefully planned dream unfold. I was our logistics officer, responsible for such key decisions as which way to aim the tent

Opposite page:
Doug Weins
crossing a
crevasse on Mt.
McKinley.

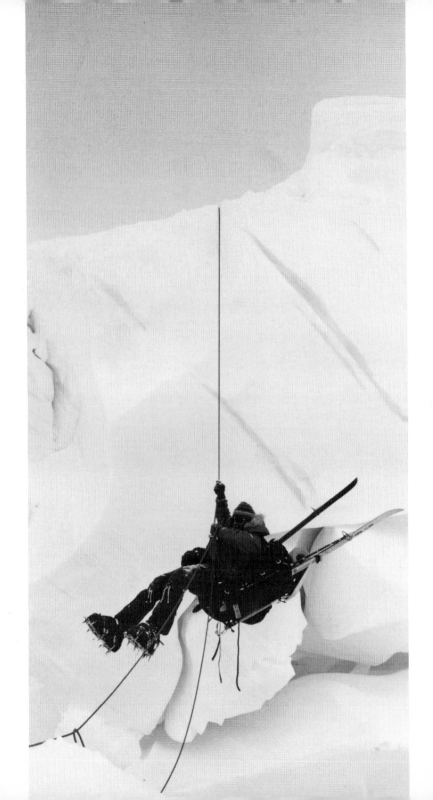

door each night. Each morning, with the consistency of the rising sun, a brisk wind blew from the exact direction the door was aimed. Alan Bard was to have been our humorist, but since everyone joked, he contributed his laughter to the general supply. Doug Weins, the lightest member of the party, quickly earned the title of chief crevasse locator. Regardless of whether he was first or last on the rope at any given time, he faithfully punched his body through the snow to discover dangerous holes for us. As it happened, he had the greatest fear of crevasses.

The East Buttress was the next major problem to overcome, and we spent six hours ascending it over 2500 feet of steep ice and snow. The route down the Ruth Glacier side was even more continuously steep, so we decided to bivouac on top rather than risk getting caught on the headwall, which averaged seventy degrees for a thousand feet. We pitched out tent on the narrow ridge crest as clouds swirled around us blocking our view. Just before sunset they lifted to reveal one of the most beautiful landscapes on earth. From an elevation of nearly 11,000 feet we looked directly across the glacier at the granite and ice of the Moose's Tooth, Mount Dickey, and Mount Huntington. The moon rose into a clear sky that turned pink, then lilac, and finally the indigo blue of an Alaskan spring night.

The next morning we made the first rappel down the headwall. It was underlain with water ice, and placing anchors was a major problem. After we left our only two ice screws behind as rappel anchors, we relied entirely on fixing the rope around bollards shoveled out of the snow cover or chopped laboriously into the ice. When the afternoon sun hit the slope, we became concerned about avalanche danger. As we neared the base and the angle lessened, Ned unroped and rushed out of reach of potential slides. Alan and I followed. Walking in our tracks, Doug dropped into a bergschrund and disappeared from sight except for the tips of his skis. It was just blind luck that the bergschrund was nearly full of snow, and Doug was able to climb out without our help. When all four of us finally stood clear of the headwall, we jumped up and down in joyful relief. On returning from the expedition, we learned that we had been the first to cross the East Buttress. A British party in 1962 had crested the ridge, only to retreat after looking down the other side.

The next day began in trepidation and ended with joyful surprises. At first we felt closed in by the peaks and icefalls that separated our arm of the Ruth Glacier from the main trunk, but after some anxious searching a skiable route opened in front of us. Nearing the great Don Sheldon Amphitheater we crossed outside the national park boundary, into the unprotected public lands then under consideration as a southern extension of the park.

Around midday as we lunched on the open glacier, two loud noises interrupted our solitude. The first was a great avalanche, falling 4000 feet and rolling half a mile across the flats before it stopped uncomfortably close to us. The second was even louder and nearer: An airplane buzzed us at fifteen feet. Now that we had entered an area where low flights and air drops were permitted, Cliff Hudson was checking our progress before leaving our final cache next to Don Sheldon's Mountain House. As the plane passed overhead, we were bombarded by falling objects marked with yellow streamers. The others rushed for cans of beer, and I found a letter from my lady in California. When I opened it, a wildflower fell out into my hand.

In the midst of this sterile landscape, the tiny flower affected me powerfully. Like animals on the hunt, mountaineers must rely almost entirely on immediate sensations. The wildflower in my hand freed my thoughts from the present and set them on a track of wild speculation; I began to see both the surrounding scene and my companions through the veil of time. I wondered if the same flower had once grown during an ancient interglacial period in the place where I now stood. Here in the Ruth Gorge was a glimpse of how the Sierra and the Rockies must have looked during the height of the Pleistocene glaciations; and the same sort of cooperative behavior that primitive man had developed for hunting and defense was evident in our group. Modern equipment couldn't hide what we left behind us each morning; a depression in the snow surrounded by tracks and droppings, not unlike the bedding area of any large mammal. Traveling this glacial world forced us to recognize our primeval heritage. I recalled John Muir's feeling of "an unexplainable mysticism" while in the presence of glaciers, and the more explicit theory of the modern biologist Valerius Geist, who discounts Africa as the major source of recent human evolution and believes that the coming of the ice in more northerly latitudes was the major factor that forced our ancestors to cooperate in groups and develop their brains.

Holding a flower on an ocean of ice, I wondered if the joy I felt in the cold, inhospitable world might be rooted in my genes. Perhaps our venture, away from our homes and loved ones over primeval valleys of ice, somehow replicated an archetypal way of human life. A sense of unfathomable nearness pulsed through me and the world closed in. Then I looked toward the Gateway to the Great Gorge. Vague images from times I never knew became intertwined with explicit memories of earlier visits to the gorge, and then the moment was gone.

Continuing on across the Ruth Glacier, we reached the Mountain House, where we spent a blissful night in the comfort of the cabin, followed by a rest day. Our second and final cache lay buried near the house in two cartons. I tore rapaciously into the first box, but Alan suggested waiting before we opened the second. On Alan's suggestion, Ned and I went off together on an afternoon ski tour to the mouth of the Gorge. We returned to a cabin brightly decorated for a surprise party. Alan and Doug had packed the second box in Ned's Vermont basement and had included all the trimmings for Ned's thirty-third birthday. Balloons, crepe streamers, and party favors hung from the ceiling. To the strains of "Happy Birthday," Ned was presented with an endless ar-

ray of things-you-always-wanted-on-a-glacier: party
hats, whistles, a toy telephone, a plastic gun that spun
tops into the air, popcorn, a cake with candles, and a
tall bottle of whiskey. Just then a group of younger
climbers on their first remote expedition happened
on the scene; they couldn't have looked more surprised had they been invited into a spaceship. The
party continued well into the night.

A day of waiting out a storm, plus two easy days
up the west fork of the Ruth Glacier, brought us to a
cul-de-sac underneath Ruth Gap, the lowest point between the Ruth and Kahiltna Glaciers. Festooned
with overhanging ice, this low point had wisely not
been called a pass. To the best of our knowledge it
had never been crossed, and it still hasn't. We opted
for a longer, less steep route that crested the South
Buttress of McKinley at 12,000 feet. Luckily we had
acquired two more ice screws from a Mount Huntington expedition; these aided our passage up a section
of 60-degree blue ice. That day ended in the middle
of a broken icefall on the Kahiltna side of the buttress. Two long overhanging rappels were necessary
to connect a route through the giant seracs. One ended hanging over space, and I had to swing back and
forth in order to sink an axe in the far wall of a deep
crevasse.

On our nineteenth day we found an easy path
through the steep lower icefall onto the east fork of
the Kahiltna Glacier. When we joined the main glacier we spotted some ski tracks that were nearly im-
perceptible until the light hit the snow at just the
right angle. It took us a while to realize that these
tracks were our own. We had closed the "Great Circle."

Our expedition lacked the great geographical cli-
max of a summit; like polar explorers, we stood in a
snowy expanse where one spot looked like the next.
Our goal was to come back to a starting point, not to
reach the heights and turn around. By itself, the
patch of snow where we stood was insignificant; what
counted was how we had come to reach it. As Ned
simply put it: "We have reached completion."

14
A
One-Day
Ascent of
Mt. McKinley

WHEN WE BECAME partners for two unique Alaskan adventures, Ned Gillette and I hardly knew each other. Chance had brought us together in Vermont when Ned had driven forty miles on a winter night to attend my lecture on high-altitude climbing. As we talked after the lecture, we both felt an unusually strong bond of understanding and trust. Ned invited me to join his ski expedition to circle Mount McKinley (described in the preceding chapter); I in turn asked him to join me immediately afterwards in an attempt to climb McKinley in a single day from its western base at 10,000 feet. Although we had no way of foreseeing it then, our mutual trust soon was to undergo an extreme test.

After the ski orbit went like clockwork, Ned and I camped at the base of McKinley's west buttress, waiting for a clear day. When it came we were off at 2:30 a.m. in the April twilight of the Alaska Range. By 5 a.m. we had reached Windy Corner at 13,400 feet where the temperature was −20° F. Instead of the soft snow I had found on a previous climb, we encountered windblown snow and patches of blue ice.

Opposite page: Ned Gillette at 16,500 feet on the west buttress of Mt. McKinley.

Just as we stopped to switch from skis to crampons, Ned's ski edges suddenly slid, and he plummeted toward a cliff, sixty feet away. Ned and I were roped together with our ice axes cleverly lashed to our packs, well out of reach. In the seconds before the rope pulled tight, I jammed the tip of a ski pole into the ice in a futile attempt at a self-arrest; then a tremendous jerk at my waist launched me toward Ned's falling form. I saw myself headed for a last, long ride in space—a vision as ghastly as Slim Pickens riding down on the bomb in the final scene of "Dr. Strangelove."

A mere arm's length from the cliff, I stopped—face first against Ned's steel ski edges. Our individual actions, unknown to each other, had cooperated to save our lives. My self-arrest had failed, but not before it slowed Ned for a split second, enabling him to grab a fixed rope left by an earlier expedition as he fell head first on his back. Adrenalin gave his gloved hand a death grip on the quarter-inch polypropylene. Had he not stopped with his skis in the air, I would have fallen past him and pulled us both off the cliff.

My hand went to my face, and my fingers felt a gaping hole where I once had a mouth. My front teeth were missing, and my lower lip was split, spread to my chin like blinders on a horse's face. With the gentle confidence that had gained my trust in Vermont, Ned said, "Don't move until we figure this out; I'm holding us with a rope in my hand behind my back."

Late that same day a plastic surgeon in Anchorage put my face back together. We had managed our own rescue by climbing and skiing twelve miles down the peak and its glaciers to a landing area for bush pilots. Once, Ned slipped into a crevasse behind me, and I pulled so hard that he popped up like toast out of a toaster.

While my injuries healed, Ned and I spent hours on the telephone between Vermont and California discussing whether we could have made the climb if the fall had not occurred. We didn't wait long to find out; a month after the accident, we returned to Mount McKinley for another try.

Normal expeditions take a month to climb the peak. What made us think we could do it so quickly? Although we were more fit than most men in their mid-thirties, we were no more so than the thousands of men, women, and children who can run twenty-six mile marathons in less than three hours. Although I run five to twelve miles of hills every day, my efforts to move my fireplug-shaped body twenty-six miles at a time never bettered three-and-a-half hours. To climb McKinley in one day, I estimated that we would need to expend the effort of four marathons back to back—sixteen to twenty hours on the move. The comparison with running cannot be taken further.

Mt. McKinley from the north: 17,000 feet of relief.

The runner has the security of knowing he can quit by simply walking off the course; the climber must find security elsewhere. Big expeditions rely on portable environments, survival equipment, and manpower. For two men with day packs on the coldest 20,000-foot peak on earth, security must come from within, from self-knowledge. Learning to combine extreme mental and physical stresses is a major reward of climbing mountains. Ned and I felt that we had the necessary blend of stamina, altitude experience, climbing skills, will power, and knowledge of the surroundings to try McKinley with no more equipment than could fit into a day pack.

Conventional expeditions move at a snail's pace because, like that animal, they carry their homes on their backs. Encumbered with hundreds of pounds per person of food, fuel, and arctic survival gear, these groups follow the tradition established by the 1913 first ascent of Mount McKinley.

The story of the first ascent is relatively uneventful, with the exception of an astonishing sight the climbers saw from the top: a flagpole stood on the summit ridge of the north peak, which is nine hundred feet lower. Three years earlier, in 1910, an Alaskan sourdough named Tom Lloyd mushed his dog team into Fairbanks, claiming that he had led his party of four from 10,000 feet to the summit of McKinley in a single day and had planted a fourteen-foot spruce flagpole on top. After an initial flurry of interest, the story was classed with legends of lost gold mines and Sasquatch sightings, but the verification of the pole by the 1913 party confirmed the tall tale as partial reality. It turned out that Lloyd had exaggerated his personal role. Weighing well over 200 pounds, he was not particularly fit, and, in fact, had never ventured over 11,000 feet. His three companions, however, had indeed gone for the summit from a camp at 10,800 feet. Charley McGonagall, reputed to be the strongest man in the North, tired of carrying the pole and quit at 18,000 feet. Billy Taylor and Pete Anderson then took the pole and reached the top of the north peak—an amazing 8500-foot climb in one day. They had spent three previous weeks shoveling and stomping a path to 16,000 feet before finally going for the top, and in this way they had inadvertently acclimatized themselves to levels well above their high camp. Their claim that they would have reached the true summit, had they known it to be higher, is entirely plausible.

If Taylor and Anderson had been credited with the true first ascent, subsequent McKinley climbs—and perhaps the entire history of American expeditionary climbing abroad—might have been based on their bold style. As it was, the sourdough's saga became a Paul Bunyan tale repeated around campfires but not in real life. For sixty-eight years, no one attempted another one-day climb from a comparable altitude. Meanwhile, more than a thousand people had reached McKinley's summit using traditional heavy expeditions and high camps.

The sourdough climb was the unwitting forerunner of the most modern style of high-altitude climbing, a sport that had moved up a blind alley for most of this century. Giant military-style expeditions hastened their own obsolescence by proving that any mountain on earth could be climbed—given enough time, equipment, money, and porter carries. The new challenge is to do great peaks in "alpine style," without fixed ropes, camps, high porters, or oxygen apparatus. An unsupported climber simply can't carry enough food and fuel to sustain himself for more than a few days on a big mountain; true alpine-style ascents must be done very fast, or not at all.

Four of the dozen highest peaks in the world have now been climbed in three days or less by fast, light expeditions. Although Mount McKinley is far lower in measured elevation than any of those, it is actually greater in vertical relief from timberline to summit. And its weather—the biggest unknown factor in any alpine-style ascent—is notoriously bad.

For two days after we had come up from sea level, Ned and I sat in the clouds at 10,000 feet, waiting for a perfect twenty-four hours of clear, still air on a peak that has the worst year-round climate of any non-polar spot on earth.

At noon on the third day the clouds lifted; the

upper mountain gleamed against blue sky. Our day had arrived rather soon, for we had counted on at least five days of acclimatization at 10,000 feet before dashing up to 20,000 feet. The forecast was for forty hours of rare calm, followed by a storm; if we let it pass, we might not get another clear spell before our ten days' supply of food and fuel ran out. On the other hand, climbing too soon could be dangerous. Our one-day time frame was far from arbitrary. The extra weight of food and fuel needed for two days would probably push the climb into a third day. Pulmonary and cerebral edema, two forms of the often fatal "climber's bends" brought on by fatigue and sudden altitude gain, almost never start until twenty-four hours after stress; and descent is a sure cure in all but the most advanced cases. To get out of the clutches of extreme altitude in a single day was sound preventive medicine. But could we move that fast without acclimatization?

Ned Gillette
catching his
breath near Mt.
McKinley's
summit.

We tried to postpone a decision and sleep a few hours but anxiety kept us wide awake. At 9 p.m. on June 9, we shouldered day packs, stepped into our skis, and struck off. We made fast time, and the sun was just setting as we reached our old 13,400-foot high point at 11 p.m. The icy traverse where we had fallen was now covered with firm snow, but without exchanging a word we cached our skis for the descent and strapped crampons onto our boots. (Ned had devised a boot combination for us utilizing oversized "Superlight" summer mountaineering boots with thin foam inners from downhill ski boots, giving us more warmth than normal double boots at a fraction of the weight.) The four-hour Alaskan night held no threat of darkness, and we continued on.

At six in the morning we took our first long rest at the standard high camp at 17,300 feet. Just below, Ned had vomited from the altitude and fatigue and was unsure about continuing, but I was eager to keep going. I started our tiny stove next to an igloo, waking two climbers who had been sleeping inside. One of them complained in a strong British accent. Hot drinks, cheese, and warmth of the sun's first rays gave Ned the strength to continue, and we left before the other climbers emerged from the igloo. We climbed for two more hours to Denali Pass at 18,200 feet, where we paused on the crest of the Alaska Range under a sky of unbroken indigo in absolutely still air.

It was a day even better than our wildest dreams, but Ned was still feeling poorly and quietly announced that he wanted to quit. My heart sank. "We'll never have another chance like this," I told him. "Only 2000 feet and we're there, and it's still early morning." He assented, and we moved on, marching like wound-down toy soldiers.

At 19,000 feet two small figures approached from below as we lay sprawled in the snow resting, all dignity abandoned. The two men stopped and eyed the obviously unfit and out-of-place climbers at their feet, and one of them remarked, "Anyone who needs a rope up here doesn't belong on this mountain!" The British accent identified him as one of the men whose sleep we had interrupted at 17,300 feet. When we introduced ourselves, their attitude became friendlier. The Britisher, Nigel Gifford, had been on expeditions to Everest and Nuptse and was planning to look me up as a climbing partner in California. His companion, John Purdue, was a Canadian. Nigel's comment about the rope had made Ned and I realize that we could do without the extra weight, so we left both rope and packs lying in the snow when we again set off. All four of us started out together, but because of Nigel and John's rest and acclimatization, Ned and I quickly were left behind. I soon began to feel like a zombie, while Ned's nausea disappeared. Our roles were being reversed and Ned was now the stronger, but our cooperative efforts kept us going.

As we neared 20,000 feet, we watched Nigel and John reach the summit, turn around, and start back down. When they stopped only a hundred feet below the top and didn't move for a long time, we wondered if something was wrong. We reached them half an hour later and found them sitting on a platform they had stamped into the steep slope, with their stove humming reassuringly in the still air. With the air of a proper British gentleman, Nigel inquired, "Would you like a cup of tea?"

We sipped and chatted for half an hour before continuing on a few minutes to the top. We were rewarded with a splendid view of the entire "Great Circle" of glaciers we had recently skied for the first time. Our climb had taken nineteen hours all told— nine for the 7300 feet to 17,300 and another nine, after a forty-five-minute rest, to make the last 3000 feet. The vertical distance we had covered was very nearly that from Mount Everest's base camp to its summit. The effort had required most of our strength, and as we started down, we moved like people with nerve injuries learning to walk—minds focused, but bodies responding with only a glimmer of their normal ability. Ned occasionally had to help me over even slight rises in the terrain, and we inevitably fell asleep during brief rests, even on steep slopes. Whoever remained conscious longer would jerk the other awake with the rope.

*Opposite page:
Ned Gillette
skiing roped
down Mt.
McKinley.*

Just before we reached the 17,300-foot camp, I checked my breathing, as I had at least once an hour since we had been above 17,000 feet. Slight gurgles in my chest indicated the beginnings of pulmonary ede-

ma; the symptoms had appeared twenty-three hours after my first exposure to increased altitude and stress—almost precisely as predicted by the experts.

The National Park Service has spent tens of thousands of taxpayers' dollars helicoptering edema victims off McKinley's upper slopes, and they advise climbers not to go too high too quickly. Statistics do show that slower parties run less risk of edema but fail to take into account the simple logic that fast, mobile parties have a far greater chance to reverse the course of the illness by prompt descent. Most rescues come after a climber has stayed in a high camp for a period of days—usually in bad weather, further delaying air rescue. We had no radio to summon a rescue and felt absolutely no need to call out, as we planned to descend quickly. When we reached high camp, we found Gifford and Purdue camped there with a large guided expedition. We were equipped to bivouac, but we gladly accepted their offer to join them for the night. Because the expedition had a radio, we decided not to mention the mild edema symptoms for fear of initiating an unnecessary rescue.

In the morning we climbed down to Windy Corner, where our skis were cached, and finished the descent with a splendid 3500-foot downhill run through icefalls and snow bowls. By the time we crawled into our tent at Kahiltna Pass, my edema had subsided. Ned and I sat watching storm clouds creep up the forty-six mile length of the Kahiltna Glacier toward the mountain, and talked about our experience. It was our first real opportunity to relax and reflect; the pace of the climb had been too intense, and we had been far too busy monitoring the weather, our progress, and our bodies.

We agreed that we owed our success on this venture—and our lives on the first attempt—to our cooperative actions, our mutual trust, and our common will. This knowledge was its own reward, and we found satisfaciton in having met the mountain on its own terms—penetrating its defenses with a few classic tools. It had not been our goal to start a speed competition on the mountain; we knew that our time would be bettered some day by people who had acclimatized longer and trained harder. We hoped that others would adopt the heritage of the sourdoughs, seeking simple ways of dealing with nature, rather than striving to overcome a mountain by a long siege. It was for this kind of experience that Ned and I had formed our partnership. Before we went to sleep, we talked of doing other fast and light expeditions in the ultimate range, the Himalaya.

15
Man
and Beast in
the Karakoram

SOME OF the earth's most splendid mountain scenery is in the Baltoro Glacier region of the Karakoram Range in northern Pakistan. Seven of the world's seventeen highest peaks encircle the Concordia Amphitheater, where glaciers pause before joining into a single stream for a thirty-mile plunge down a granite canyon that makes Yosemite seem like a city park. Although the single peak of Mount Everest is taller, this region—a thousand miles to the northwest—has the world's highest mean elevation. Another feature that sets it apart from most mountain areas of exceptional beauty is that it has no legal protection whatsoever.

We Americans have a long history of isolationism, and although it has dwindled from our politics, it still haunts our environmental thinking. Many of us are lulled into a false confidence that certain areas will remain pristine because of their geographical remoteness. I thought so until I trekked two hundred fifty miles round trip to K2, the 28,250-foot culmination of the Karakoram Himalaya.

I had dreamed of visiting the Karakoram ever

Opposite page: George Schaller near the toe of the Baltoro Glacier, Pakistan.

149

since I began mountain climbing in my teens. Over campfires in the Sierra Nevada, I found others who shared the same image: a light, self-contained expedition which would not get involved with high summits that required oxygen and hundreds of native porters. A phone call erased that image in an instant. I was offered a place on the 1975 American K2 Expedition. The choice was clear-cut: to go or stay home.

In April 1975, ten of us sat in an ancient high-ceilinged hotel room in Rawalpindi, Pakistan. We were waiting for a daily-scheduled flight to Skardu in Pakistan-held Kashmir, the embarkation point for the Karakoram. We had begun to realize why PIA airlines was locally called "Perhaps I Arrive," or "Please Inform Allah." The cloud-shy pilots fly only in perfect weather, so the flight was delayed eleven days. Stacked in the corner of the large room were dozens of five-gallon tins of rancid butter, purchased for our six hundred porters at a cost of over $700. We were discussing the $2000 cost of our government-required porter insurance when someone knocked at the door.

A tall slender man dressed in American clothes entered the room. We had never seen him before. He asked if our expedition had someone named Dr. Schaller. We replied that Robert T. Schaller was our expedition doctor. He said, "My name is Dr. Schaller, too. I've been getting phone calls from a young lady I do not know in the United States. She's on the phone right now, in the hotel lobby." Rob Schaller, a marathon runner, shot out the door as if he had heard a starter's pistol. The new Dr. Schaller turned to leave. Something clicked in my head, but I thought, no, it couldn't be; this is too young to have done all that. The man I'm thinking of must be seventy.

Leif Patterson, a step ahead of me, asked the new Dr. Schaller if he was by chance the zoologist, George B. Schaller, who had written *The Year of the Gorilla* and *The Serengeti Lion*. Modestly, he answered "Yes," then departed nearly as quickly as his namesake.

Curiosity got the best of me and I visited George

Schaller in his hotel room that evening. I learned that he planned to follow our same route, walking two hundred miles round trip up the Baltoro Glacier nearly to the base of K2. Because our expedition might disturb what he had come to study, he had planned to go ahead of us, but had also been held back by the flight.

Looking about the empty room I asked him where all his provisions were. He would be traveling over glaciers at high altitude far beyond the highest village. He pointed to a small box on the floor that contained about twenty pounds of nuts and meats. Only one porter and a Pakistani friend would accompany him. His object was to survey large mammals in the K2 region and assess the need for a national park as proposed by the government. K2 is possibly the most remote high mountain on earth, not visible from any inhabited spot. Why would such a place need the protection a national park could offer? Schaller wasn't sure that it did, but he realized that time was running out for the once-remote mountains. More people had visited the Himalayas in the last decade than in all preceding history.

K2 and the Baltoro Glacier region missed this on-slaught because the area was closed for political reasons from 1961 to 1974. Through no intent or fore-thought—most probably because of the lack of it—the government of Pakistan held the region back in time, saving it from clashes with modern culture. Now, a year after the floodgates were opened in 1974, nineteen expeditions had permission to travel the same route toward the Baltoro. While they would cer-tainly bring back new aesthetic and topographic infor-mation, they would do little to illuminate other con-cerns more basic to establishing a park. How much pristine flora and fauna are left to save? Does human habitation in the valleys make the concept of a park untenable? Who would benefit? Who would lose? Schaller's tiny expedition had a better chance of an-swering these questions than all the others combined, but as I talked to him in his hotel room, I wondered if we each might have our special brand of blinders. I

would be marching straight toward K2 in a caravan of
six hundred, as insulated from the true environment
as a politician touring a ghetto in a limousine, while
Schaller would walk the narrow path of science, ren-
dering unfathomable splendor into a jargon of numbers and words.

I couldn't have been more wrong. At first,
Schaller's world seemed closed to me. He answered
questions like a computer; just what I expected from a
dedicated scientist. Then he began to quiz me:

"What route are you trying on K2?"

"The West Ridge. It's unclimbed, you know."

"Oh. That's on the other side of the mountain
from the Italian route. You must be going up the
Godwin-Austen Glacier, then up the Savoia very near
the Chinese border."

"Exactly. Our route lies directly on the border.
How do you know so much about the mountain?
You're supposed to be a zoologist, not a climber."

"I've read a lot about the expeditions. I used to
climb some myself."

Now in his early forties, Schaller's interests
seemed as diverse as a child's. He had a healthy sense
of wonder; he yearned to travel into Tibet, but had
been turned down by the Chinese. He had studied the
relationships between predators and prey in India, especially the tiger and the deer, and had made three
prior visits to the Karakoram, once taking the only
photographs of snow leopards ever made in the wild.
Eating *chapatties* in a native village was far less foreign
to him than reclining in a comfortable chair in acade-
mia.

What separated Schaller from most adventurers
was his keen intellect. He assumed nothing unless he
confirmed the facts for himself, thus avoiding the
common plight of building a false pyramid of logic on
top of someone else's misconception. At the same
time, he would not quickly dismiss a statement just because it was not backed by a verified fact. Instead he
would tuck it into his mind; a new avenue to investi-
gate if the chance arose. He professed what was her-
esy to many wildlife managers: "It is sometimes neces-

sary for radical protective measures to precede, rather than follow, scientific studies and surveys."

Pakistan was a classic example. Wildlife research was at least forty years behind North America. Local universities were not ecologically oriented and Schaller believed that wildlife officials worked almost in an intellectual vacuum. "I met no one who knew details of the wildlife-research program in neighboring Iran," he mused. "I work mainly with large mammals not just because they are my specialty, but also because their status and condition normally indicate the concern with which a country treats its natural resources. In Pakistan, a great number of animals are on the threshold of extinction."

The night before I met Schaller, I had dined with a Pakistani who seemed most knowledgeable about local wildlife. When I asked about the Abominable Snowman, he laughed in open contempt. Schaller fielded the same question entirely differently:

> I don't know whether such a creature exists, but if it does it will be found in the forested regions between Nepal and Bhutan rather than in the arid Karakoram. I've studied photographs of the tracks and there are characteristics that have not yet been explained to my satisfaction. Some of them may be melted-out tracks of smaller animals, or of bears, but others have subtle things in common with gorilla tracks; things that no one could fake unless they had spent years studying primates. I'm not saying that the Abominable Snowman is a gorilla; quite to the contrary, but the latent similarities intrigue me. I would not be that surprised if an undiscovered large primate exists in very low numbers.

A few days later, Schaller joined us on a chartered flight to Skardu. We crossed the moist Western Himalaya near Nanga Parbat, then watched the terrain plunge downward for 23,000 feet into the canyon of the Indus River, the largest land escarpment on earth. Beyond, the Karakoram swelled in an endless sea of white caps rising from arid valleys into the clouds. In the distance, K2 rose high above the others, a perfect pyramid hoisted on the shoulders of giants.

Only ten of our twelve tons of gear were on the flight, so we waited an extra week for another plane. Meanwhile, Schaller went about his survey, inviting me to join him one day. We rode with Pakistani wildlife managers to a nearby valley that was reported to have ibex—large wild goats that inhabit mountains in Europe, North Africa, and Asia. Not far beyond the end of the jeep road, the officials stopped to go fish-

A Balti
herdsman.

ing. Schaller and I continued, hiring a native boy to help us spot wildlife. When Schaller drank from a stream, I noticed that his posture was exactly like one of the big cats he had studied so long, a hint that he was somewhat more than a passive observer.

My image of lush mountain valleys dimmed after he told me that this valley, Shagarthang, was characteristic of the Karakoram. Insulated from the monsoon by the Western Himalaya, it was practically treeless, except for planted orchards and shade trees, and a few scattered junipers. The main wild growth was sagebrush and *ephedra*, similar to species found in the high deserts of the American West. Cultivation extended beyond 10,000 feet, and livestock grazed much higher, usurping almost all the available wildlife habitat. In summer, ibex could graze steep meadows up to 18,000 feet, but their population was limited by the need to descend into lower valleys in winter, where they were often shot if they didn't starve. Even with these problems, the ibex were doing better than many other species.

The snow leopard, one of the rarest of big cats, has the Achilles heel of eating its dinner slowly. With prey greatly depleted, they often resort to domestic sheep and goats. Many, while savoring their last supper, are killed by villagers. Others are shot for their valuable furs. There may be more skins for sale in city bazaars than live animals left in the mountains. Schaller estimated that only two hundred fifty survived in all of Pakistan.

He told me that existing government controls were a series of paradoxes. There were large forest departments but few forests. There were strict laws against killing large mammals in the Karakoram, but almost no enforcement. One of the Skardu officials openly traveled with a rifle and had recently shot nine ibex and eight mountain sheep.

The day ended without seeing a single large mammal other than domestic yaks, sheep, and goats, but for Schaller it was not a failure. He questioned villagers carefully and gained considerable information on wildlife in the valley. To test them, he had thrown out a few curves about species that were not present. If they passed the quiz, he placed some credence in their reports.

While we waited for our remaining equipment, Schaller began the long trek up the Braldu River toward the Baltoro. Weeks later, we met him near the glacier's snout. Excitedly, I told him about photographing a band of ibex from a few hundred feet away. He asked me for exact details, then told me that I had seen a species of urial mountain sheep; ibex have bigger horns and a grander appearance. Like a trophy hunter, I was disappointed. It was some consolation that urial were rarer. Fewer than 1,000 existed in all of Pakistan. Related to the Rocky Mountain sheep, they were built more like an antelope, and they avoided danger by speed rather than climbing cliffs.

Schaller told me of his own disappointment. According to the Pakistan Forest Department there were 4,500 ibex, 2,500 shapu, and 450 musk deer in the 1,600 square kilometers of proposed park. His survey of the heart of the same region indicated only about 100 each of ibex and urial with no sign of musk deer. He thought the department's figures were up to ten times too high. The low prey population supported very few predators. He found only old, faint signs of snow leopards and wolves plus the fresh tracks of one brown bear and several foxes. He never saw most of the high peaks because it had stormed every day. It was his opinion that the Baltoro Glacier was the ugliest in the world, and he seriously questioned whether much would be gained by creating a national park. Access was too difficult for most vistors, and wildlife could more easily be protected by stationing a game warden in the highest village. The urial needed special attention to survive, but this could be done without park status.

As he shouldered his pack to leave, he said, "If you want to try your hand at photographing ibex, there's a large herd above Liliwa, next to the glacier. They're very hard to approach."

Walking across the Baltoro I agreed with him. Completely covered with dark heaps of loose rock, it

Opposite page:
Siberian ibex
above the Baltoro
Glacier.

was certainly the ugliest glacier I had ever seen. The weather was still stormy, and I saw little of the mountains. Passing all that beauty hiding in the mist was as frustrating as being blindfolded on a tour of the Louvre.

I reached Liliwa camp long before the porters, and there, thousands of feet above, were ibex walking across steep snow. I climbed to within a few hundred yards of the animals at nearly 15,000 feet. I counted fifteen, and they were definitely aware of my presence. I tried not to exceed their toleration of closeness. When I moved a few feet nearer, they would group to retreat, but when I stayed back and pretended to ignore them, they would return to feeding on dead grasses buried under shallow snows. I watched them for several hours.

I knew avalanches were a major cause of ibex deaths, but was amazed how much their behavior resembled that of trained mountaineers and cross-country skiers. They crossed steep snow one at a time and moved vertically rather than horizontally in areas of great danger, so that their paths did not bisect the slopes. Even their daily activity cycle had adapted: they rested on ledges during the warm, dangerous hours of the afternoon. I plotted a way to get a closer look by forcing them toward a steep rock wall that could be climbed by a snow ramp leading back toward me. If they took the bait, they would climb to a ridge profiled against the sky nearly twice as close as their normal tolerance. I would try to get photos with a 500mm lens.

One by one the ibex climbed the ramp to a rock outcrop. There they regrouped and started for the next outcrop, does in the lead, youngsters in the middle, and bucks bringing up the rear. The first ibex reached the crest of the ridge, looked down at me, then disappeared around the corner. Each animal took its turn while I shot a roll of film in a minute or two. Here were animal counterparts of human mountaineers. Their ancestors had forsaken a more predictable but mundane existence in the valleys for an active alpine life filled with dangers. I felt a strong kinship, and as evening neared I regretted having to descend to the noisy camp.

The next morning, not far from camp, the large tracks of a snow leopard paralleled our route. They were only hours old, and although I never saw the animal I felt something of its presence from the prints in the snow. They symbolized a bond with times not long ago when men, too, walked barefoot on the ice. I thought of the special attraction that recently glaciated valleys held for me, and realized that my emotions were dependent on finding bonds with things in my past. It was like returning to a forgotten street of my youth. Where things were changed and old buildings gone, there would be a dull ache, but it would take only a familiar tree or a crack in a sidewalk to make happiness flow into my life. In the Karakoram, much of that happiness came from meeting adversity and observing how it had shaped things. Was it my imagination, or did I see hidden similarities between the arc of a side glacier, the curl of an ibex horn, and the twisting grain of a juniper, all hewn by the same wind, cold, and snow that were now acting on my own body? I knew Schaller had felt comparable emotions when he wrote, "The mountains will remain magnificent even without wildlife, but when the last snow leopard disappears from the icy crags, an intangible aura of mystery will vanish too."

This is the essence of what must be preserved by national parks: unstructured wildness where people can imagine their own destinies.

Schaller and I returned home with perceptions of the Karakoram enhanced by our own special interests. I was disappointed not to have climbed K2 and his wildlife Shangri-La had not proved to be a reality. His memories were dominated by glimpses of animals moving against a misty backdrop of mountains. Mine were of cold and sterile peaks in which wildlife decorated the foreground. These were not opposite viewpoints, but rather subtle shifts of the same basic impressions.

In a similar way, we differed on the park proposal. Schaller recognized that scenic grandeur alone

A caravan of 600 marching toward K2.

would qualify the K2 region for park status, but his biological orientation made him question whether this was the place for a park. He believed that other areas of the Karakoram might be more suitable "as last refuges for animals and plants, as repositories of genetic stock in the event that some day the species may be needed to revitalize this plundered land."

I still hold to the belief that national parks should be shrines celebrating the grandest works of nature. The view from the Concordia Amphitheater exceeds anything in McKinley, Yosemite, or Grand Canyon parks. Nothing I have ever seen compares with one spring night spent at Concordia, when the cloud curtain rose after a storm and the moon shone on a vast, circular stage of incredible peaks.

Unfortunately, another extreme is also present within the proposed park boundaries. Unlike Schaller, I found no scarcity of large mammals. One species, my own, dominated all the others. Nineteen groups composed of up to 600 individuals far exceeded the meager resources of the lower valleys. Unlike other wildlife, these feral creatures had an apparent defect in their social mechanisms that lowered the carrying capacity of their habitat by concentrating them in the same places, which became quickly denuded of vegetation. Traveling with the largest group, I once observed the result of a three-day layover in one locale. The earth, the water, and the smell of the air were polluted by more than a thousand fresh piles of excrement! This barren, brown battlefield was but a wafting on the first breeze of a human tornado yet to come. The Pakistani government forbids airdrops or airlifts, thus ensuring that mass human impact will continue to increase. For the journey to the base of K2, porters must carry their own food for ten days beyond the highest village. By government regulation, they are allotted two pounds of food per day and a maximum of a fifty-five pound load. In perfect weather, with no porter strikes, such as we experienced, and with only half rations for the return, more porters would have to be hired to carry food than to carry expedition loads.

The problems of preservation in wildlands that have native residents are extremely complex. They cannot be solved within the normal concept of a national park. Either that concept must be modified into an overall plan to fit the K2 region, or proper measures must be undertaken individually, which seems unlikely at best. One thing seems certain: remoteness alone will no longer do the job. What is at stake is not just another frontier, but one of our planet's final strongholds.

16
Topping the
Trango Towers

ON THE WAY to K2 in 1953 Bob Craig saw the Trango Towers from the Baltoro Glacier. "These are hardly mountains," he later wrote, "they are fantasies of the imagination. . . blocks of rock, often capped with ice, rise vertically for 8000 feet, for all the world like mammoth skyscrapers."

Even after this call to arms, the Trangos went untouched for another two decades. Mountaineers recognized that the world's greatest granite peaks were in the K2 region, but they were prevented from attempting them because of Indo-Pakistani politics. Meanwhile, the sport of mountaineering evolved more within those years than during the entire preceding century. During the years of the Karakoram closure, the distinctive mark of expedition mountaineering shifted away from simply achieving altitude toward style. Joe Brown, the best British rock climber of his generation, made first ascents of Kangchenjunga and Mustagh Tower in the mid-fifties, but instead of turning his sights toward other big peaks, Brown put the Trango Towers at the top of his list.

Opposite page: Great Trango Tower, Karakoram, Pakistan. Route follows left center of face.

163

In 1974 the Karakoram reopened, and Dennis Hennek organized an American expedition to the Trangos. I was invited, but I opted to go to K2 instead when permission for the Trangos went to Brown's six-man expedition. As the huge K2 effort floundered on the approach march, due to bad weather and porter strikes, I longed for the simple joy of a small expedition to the Trango Towers with a few friends. I had no clear mountain views until midway along the Baltoro Glacier. There I awoke to the sounds of a Beethoven concerto on a tape deck, as the sun's first light struck the Towers. Like a branding iron held against the sky, they rose from a common base into distinctive forms of naturally red granite that held a crimson glow.

The first tower was a castle roofed with ice, flanked by an exquisite, flawless spire culminating in a bird's beak. Then came the Great Trango Tower, a matriarch in flowing robes, at once sheer and portly. Beyond, and partly veiled in cloud, was Nameless Tower, the goal of Brown's expedition, a youthful, slim pinnacle that stayed relentlessly vertical during its final half-mile thrust. Nameless, a non-name, suggested a feature too eternal to be defined by mere mortals. Not one of this array of summits had been reached, but their time was growing near. Returning from K2 on the flight from Skardu to Rawalpindi I sat with Joe Brown's expedition, going home after a failure on the Trangos. Six hundred feet from the 20,500-foot summit, Martin Boysen had jammed his knee in a crack. After hours of agony his buddies brought up bivouac gear so that he could hang all night in some comfort. That inspired him toward a more drastic measure. He used a knife to cut away his thick pants from his knee, piece by piece. His knee came out bleeding and battered; the expedition, already far behind schedule, retreated.

By 1977, when we received permission to return to the Karakoram, a number of the region's granite peaks had been climbed, including Nameless Tower, but the Great Trango Tower remained virgin. My photographs of it showed a superb natural line as-

cending the southwest face in a bold "Z." I hoped our
six-man expedition could climb it alpine style, without
fixed ropes or relaying of loads. To do an unclimbed
Trango Tower with simplicity and speed seemed to us
the ultimate joy in Himalayan adventure.

On the morning of July 19, 1977, I headed up a
3500-foot couloir with a sixty-pound pack as fast as I
could go. The couloir led to a col separating the
Great Trango from the first tower, and it acted as an
avalanche funnel for the massive south faces of both
peaks. We camped under the Trangos for five days,
and on every one of them gargantuan slides of rock
and snow swept the couloir. I felt like a snail on a city
sidewalk, carrying my home on my back in the presence of forces that could squash me without warning.

One trip up the gully: that was all; one trip that
the six of us planned never to repeat again; one trip
with everything we needed for an alpine-style climb.

We rushed the couloir when the odds were with
us in the cool of the morning. When the sun struck
the face, the safety catch would unfreeze on untold
tons of poised rock and snow, ready to explode without warning down the gunbarrel we were ascending.
Four of us reached the 17,000-foot col within minutes
of one another, taking less than four hours to move
3500 vertical feet with heavy loads at altitude—a sus-
tained physical output equivalent to running a marathon. We four were equals, the best-matched foursome I'd ever climbed with. But we wouldn't have
been on the Trango Towers were it not for the other
two climbers, still in the dangerous couloir long past
noon.

Dennis Hennek was a carpenter, John Roskelley
a geologist, Kim Schmitz an unemployed ski bum, and
I a free-lance writer. Between us, we didn't even have
the funds to cover our air tickets. Below us were doctors Jim Morrissey and Lou Buscaglia. Jim had led the
1973 American Dhaulagiri Expedition and had future plans for K2 in 1979. He wanted to see K2 first-
hand, so both he and his friend Lou paid more than
their fair share of costs to make our expedition a
reality.

We busied ourselves making a tent platform while waiting apprehensively for the two doctors. None of us was selfless; no one volunteered to go back into the danger zone and help them with their loads. At two in the afternoon the four of us saw our worst fear realized. A tremendous avalanche roared 6000 feet down the face of the Great Trango, missed our protected col, and swept the couloir clean. We yelled down. No answer. A fresh tongue of sickening white snow curved out of sight, trackless and as empty as our hearts.

No one discussed descending. We intuitively followed the "Aleister Crowley rescue principle." After a 1905 Kangchenjunga expedition, Crowley had been ostracized by the British climbing establishment because he continued afternoon tea when his companions were buried by an avalanche. He reasoned that he had warned them not to be on that slope after midday; if they were in trouble, he wasn't about to risk his life for those already dead. And they did die.

Our situation differed because Jim and Lou had done nothing wrong except follow our mutual desire to climb the tower. The couloir's danger was a proven fact, and we four had proceeded every man for himself. Jim was the only one of us acting selflessly; he had stayed back to help his slower friend. What were we to do?

The obstacles that we had overcome to reach the Trango now seemed futile. I remembered dashing through Rawalpindi trying to replace items lost in transit by Lufthansa. And our worry when all communications were severed due to a military coup. And Mohammed Hussain, our chief porter, who missed a jeep because our liaison officer gave him the wrong departure time, walked sixty miles without food or sleep to catch us in less than a day; Mohammed, who had carried frostbitten George Bell a hundred miles from K2 on his back in 1953; Mohammed who had carried our stricken K2 high porter, Akbar, along the Godwin-Austen Glacier as a 50-year-old man in 1975; Mohammed, who now waited at a camp below the couloir with concern etched into his features.

I remembered double-staging in two days what were normally four days of travel, offering porters extra benefits. When they asked for fresh meat on the Glacier, I had made a proposition: we would buy the biggest goat in the high village and march it on a leash for two days. If we got to the four-day campsite, the porters would eat the goat; if not, the climbers would feast instead. At the end of a day we came to a wide torrent spanned by a rope bridge in an advanced state of decay. Many of the porters refused to cross with their loads. Their leaders solemnly announced that the goat would have to be eaten on the spot. We argued to no avail; until suddenly the porters stopped and stared in awe as John carried the goat across the bridge on his own back! The next evening we camped in sight of the Trango Towers while the porters dined on goat.

John Roskelley carrying a live goat across a swinging vine bridge.

We had made the fastest expedition approach
march to the Baltoro Glacier in history, but what did
that mean now? We had been powered by a constant
state of optimistic expectation during those miracu-
lous seven days from Rawalpindi to base camp. Today,
dread was taking its place.

The afternoon lingered in suspended animation.
The spell broke toward evening when we heard voices
in the couloir. I felt as if the world's largest pack had
been lifted from my shoulders. The doctors had
heard the slide coming and had scrambled up the
sidewall of the couloir moments before it swept past.

I realized that safety, health, and happiness were
far more important than any summit. I wondered if
the doctors should continue. Fatigued and blistered,
Lou made his own decision to wait at the col until we
came down from the climb. Jim wanted to go with us
and offered to descend if necessary. I never figured
out how this might have been accomplished. On the
other hand, how could we deny a place on the team to
a healthy member who had made it all possible? Jim
trusted us and knew what he was getting into. He was
a fit, experienced mountaineer who lacked our years
spent on big rock walls. I realized that it took more
courage for him to follow us up the Trango without
our background than it did for us to lead the way using techniques that were as second nature to us as
driving a car.

Before dawn, after a still and clear night, we said
goodbye to Lou and shouldered packs that looked disturbingly small and felt disturbingly heavy. Kim and I
took lighter loads than the others because we were
leaders for the day. We would alternate pitches and
fix ropes for the others. They would follow on jumar
ascenders, pull out the ropes, and bring them to us so
that we could continue leading.

Sunrise caught us near the base of a steep rock-
band where Kim was leading an ice-filled 5.8 crack in
the best alpine granite we had ever seen. He moved
with slow grace and confidence, belying the effort he
was expending to lieback a crack in double boots at
18,000 feet. We were in ecstasy; the weather, the

rock, the surroundings, and the companionship were all as fine as we could ever desire. When I reached Kim in the middle of a headwall, we looked at each other and giggled with delight.

Kim Schmitz leading a 5.8 pitch in mountain boots at 18,000 feet on the Trango Tower.

When it was my lead I had the choice of beginning a long headwall that would take all day, or veering left to a steep snow and ice ramp. The headwall would be safe for now, but it had a potential long-range threat. How long could we expect the weather to hold? I knew from 1975 that our fine rock could disappear under a crust of ice during a serious summer storm. The snow ramp offered speed, but it led past the chute that had spilled yesterday's monster avalanche. I gambled on getting beyond the chute before the morning thaw.

For a tense two hours we pitted our speed against the rising sun. Then we reached the safety of a ridge-crest and ate lunch. The source of the avalanches was now above us, a long ice field covered with a thin layer of snow. We chose an area that had already slid and headed up what appeared to be a 500-foot beeline to a giant ledge. The distance proved to be 1500 feet and the ledge was nonexistent. We found a narrow,

corniced crest overhanging a 6000-foot drop to the
Dunge Glacier. It was separated from the main wall
by a wide gap. There was no other bivouac site, so we
dug a tiny platform into the cornice. Just under the
snow was blue ice that took hours to chop away with
out axes. We had no tent, so we tied ourselves to a
safety rope anchored to ice screws and scrunched
close together on ensolite pads.

Dinner was a great disappointment. We discovered that much of our food had been accidently left at
the col. The single stove refused to work properly and
it took an hour to warm a pot of water. After a meager meal we counted what was left for two more days
of climbing: three packets of hot chocolate, six tea
bags, one packet of soup, a half-pound of cheese, and
two bacon bars. No one complained. Although the
lack of food was due in part to an oversight, we had
always planned to go as light as possible high on the
peak. No one expected much in comforts, so no one
was disturbed to have a bit less. Had we decided on
normal expeditionary tactics, thousands of feet of
rope would have been fixed and two tents would have
been dug into the cornice. We would have had at least
two stoves, several days of extra food, and possibly a
radio to talk to base. And we would have taken the
very essence of mountaineering, something primitive
and uncivilized, and channelled it into a highly
evolved situation totally dependent on civilized goods
and long-range plans.

On the Trango Tower our civilized trappings
were at a minimum. A few classic tools and supplies,
that was all. We felt connected to the mountain rather
than to a rope-and-camp system attached to the
mountain. And although we were isolated from the
world, we felt perfectly in control of our destinies.

We awoke at our 19,000-foot bivouac while stars
were still shining and the snowy landscape was locked
in the phosphorescent blue of night. As we packed
our loads for the summit push, we were treated to a
special high-altitude light show. Shadows of the Karakoram giants were cast into the stratosphere against
the purple pre-dawn gloaming. Before sun hit the

peaks we rappelled down to the ice field, leaving our bivouac gear on the platform.

A traverse across the top of the ice field brought us left of the cleft that had separated our bivouac from the main wall. We chose a deep rock chimney filled with ice, and I hung for long hours from a piton as Dennis and John led upward. Wearing crampons to climb thin ice over rock, it took seven hours to make only 600 feet.

In the middle of the afternoon we reached an ice ramp that led to the summit ridge, where an awesome cornice blocked the route. I worried about time; in order to return to the bivouac by dark, we would soon have to turn around whether we had made the top or not.

Dennis gained the summit ridge by an easy notch hidden at the edge of the cornice. Soon all five of us were walking along the narrow crest toward the highest point. We were surrounded by giant peaks in late afternoon light, all in familiar positions save one. Nameless Tower, marked on most maps as the highest of the Trangos, was already below us before the final rise to the summit. Apparently surveyors had measured the highest point of the Great Trango visible from the foot of the Baltoro Glacier, a rock spire several hundred feet lower than the snow dome that was the true summit. Unknowingly we were making the first ascent of the highest Trango.

On top we hugged each other with supreme joy. The air was absolutely still and we stripped off jackets and gloves. Glaciers and peaks extended out from us in all directions, and for a few minutes we felt as if we were in the center of the universe, perched on a cloud. We might have rolled in the snow and burst out laughing with complete emotional release, were it not for the prospect of the descent, always in our minds.

After half an hour on top we started down. Rappels, interminable rappels, set up by two, descended by five, retrieved by two, then reset by the first two. Darkness caught us on the ice field traverse after one of our ropes had been left behind on a jammed rap-

pel. We fixed our remaining three ropes to ice screws, kept going in the blackness, and got to the platform with just a few feet to spare at ten o'clock.

By the next afternoon we were free of the couloir. Only then did we feel full satisfaction and freedom to celebrate. Mohammed Hussain greeted us with open arms at base camp. We reveled in level ground, flowers, wash water, and most of all in food. The best thing about lightweight adventuring is that it makes you realize how very fine the smaller things of life really are. From a duffle we pulled out goodies that we had been saving and prepared a victory dinner of shrimp cocktail, hot tea, mashed potatoes with butter and chives, fried beef patties, rose cabernet, cognac, and blueberry pie.

Only twenty-four days after we had begun, we returned to Rawalpindi, still in ecstasy over a tiny expedition that lacked all the inescapable ballyhoo of big mountain sagas.

Opposite page: The summit of Great Trango Tower. Broad Peak and the Gasherbrums on horizon.

17
Skiing the
Karakoram
High Route

MY EXPEDITION dreams have almost always failed, not in the field on some windswept ridge where the elements proved too strong for human powers, but around a campfire in the Sierra or the desert where an idea flickered out with the embers. The pattern has been nearly always the same. Random talk of mountains and people becomes specific. An image of a light, self-contained expedition to the Himalaya forms. Just good friends and good climbing. Big efforts with oxygen and lots of porters are out. The magnet is that time on the mountain, working together toward a meaningful goal, isolated from the rest of humanity and any need to depend upon it for success or enjoyment.

The magnet has an opposite, equally forceful pole. All Himalayan climbing expeditions include a lot of time in the mountains that is not one's own. The shorter and more efficient the climb itself, the greater the proportion of time spent in the lowlands dealing and living with a basically unwanted caravan of men and supplies. Where air drops, vehicle access, or pack animals can be utilized, it is still possible to

Opposite page: Dan Asay on Nordic skis at 21,000 feet, above Conway Saddle.

175

climb without coming face to face with one's own he-
donism, but in the Himalayas, where each hour of
mountain pleasure can be equated with days of toil by
hired hands, the dream around a campfire is never
fulfilled. When the embers go out, they leave a subtle
division of minds. On the one hand are those who will
not compromise their ideals. They stay to pursue
simpler goals in accessible ranges. On the other hand
are those like myself, who sell their dreams short for a
little instant gratification and experience.

My solution to this conflict is as simple as it is absurd. If the root of the problem is all that gear needed
to climb a mountain, why climb a mountain at all?
With this non-objective firmly in mind, I organized
the 1980 American Karakoram Traverse Expedition.
Our goal was to traverse the highest range on earth,
the Karakoram Himalaya, across northern Pakistan
from the Indian border three-fourths of the way to
Afghanistan. We would follow the greatest of all the
world's high routes, an aesthetic line over four of the
largest glaciers outside the subpolar latitudes. This
pathway of ice doglegs from glacier to glacier, yet in
an overall way it follows a remarkable east-to-west
trend through the very heart of the range. From the
high perspective of satellite photos taken in summer,
the blue glaciers rest on a tawny landscape like long
beads strung on a loose necklace. In the winter and
spring, however, all is hidden under snow. After the
shortest days of winter were past, but long before the
snow melted from the highlands, our four-man expedition would set out on Nordic skis with small sleds.
We hoped to become the first expedition to move
through the heart of the Himalaya under its own
power, and to capture something of our elusive
dreams.

On March 27th we began our two-hundred-
eighty-five-mile traverse from the village of Khapalu

at the confluence of the Shyok and Saltoro rivers. Ten
porters were hired to take us to the snowline, from
where we would strike out on our own, with just one
food cache in the village of Askole, a short distance
off our route between the Baltoro and Biafo glaciers.

Otherwise, we would travel entirely above human habitation. Each man would have one hundred twenty pounds. We could find no way to go lighter. Besides food and survival gear for weeks of sub-zero living, we needed considerable fuel to melt snow for water, climbing gear to traverse the south face of Sia Kangri at 22,500 feet between the Siachen and Baltoro basins, durable ski equipment, and ropes for protection against crevasse falls.

Our foursome consisted of Dan Asay, Ned Gillette, Kim Schmitz, and myself. We set off up the Bilafond Glacier, feeling very alone as the porters retreated. Here, just a few miles from the Indian border, we planned to cross the 18,000-foot Bilafond La and follow the Lolofond Glacier to its juncture with the Siachen. It had proved politically impossible to begin in India on the snout of the Siachen itself.

The conditions were extremely gratifying. No one had been on these great glaciers in winter and we had been given every conceivable prediction. One geographer told Ned to expect unconsolidated powder several feet deep at high altitude. What we found was a steady, firm surface. It was too cold to form a crust, yet windblown enough to allow the leader to break trail almost as fast as the others could follow.

Cold was our enemy on the Siachen. The basin of over four hundred square miles of gently sloping ice was a perfect trap for temperature inversions. In the populated Saltoro Valley the temperature never dropped below 20°F at 11,000 feet, but at 16,000 on the Siachen we found ourselves trying to pass a −25° F night with light sleeping bags rated above zero.

For me, the greatest hardship to this point was not the huge loads or the icy winds, but the simple act of rushing out of the tent with full bowels on that coldest dawn. My hasty motions dislodged hoar frost from every panel of the dome tent, dusting Kim and me with a thick layer of ice. For the first time in decades, I thought about the old crystal paperweight that used to sit on my father's desk. When I was a child, I turned it over in my hands and watched artificial snow fall on the hapless figure inside. I used to imag-

ine how small, cold, and insignificant that little man
felt in a world beyond his control. On the Siachen,
surrounded by bleak and foreign peaks, I became that
little man.

Our travel up the glacier was ritualistic rather
than eventful. We gained about a thousand feet each
day, spending only about five hours out of twelve actually skiing. Two hours were used to break camp, and
two more to set it up. Frequent rest stops ate up another three hours. Our effort was not much greater
than it would have been with lighter loads. We just
moved far slower with sixty pounds on our backs, fifty
on a children's roll-up vinyl sled, and ten more in a
reversed fanny pack.

On the afternoon of April 12th, we reached the
Siachen's end. Though our maps had warned us of
what was coming, we were surprised to watch our gentle plateau disappear into a Grand Canyon-sized
chasm. A vertical mile below us was the head of the
Kondus Glacier, and just a mile and a half across from
us was Conway Saddle, hanging into space like the
abutment of a collapsed bridge.

Here was the gap that had stopped the Work-
mans and other turn-of-the-century explorers from
traversing between the Baltoro and Siachen basins.
Not until 1979 was a crossing finally made, and then
by a fully equipped Japanese expedition with 116 porters that had just made an ascent of Sia Kangri.

We planned to follow their route, traversing the
south face of Sia Kangri between 20,500 and 22,500
feet. The fact that the Japanese had made their traverse with full equipment and portage in summer did
little for my confidence that we could follow the same
route on Nordic skis in winter conditions. Ned was
convinced that we would find easier going than on
our Nordic circumambulation of Mount McKinley,
and his hunch proved right.

It took three days and several rappels to make
the mile-and-a-half traverse, but the true story was in
what it didn't take. We never switched to our crampons, and we never encountered hard ice except going down on rappel. The route just opened up in

front of us as we went. Each portentous obstacle had a reasonable alternative, hidden from view until the last moment.

Both Kim and I had been to the Baltoro region on two previous expeditions. We began to see familiar landmarks in the distance. Mustagh Tower loomed into the golden light of dawn from the same horrendous perspective made famous by Vittorio Sella's 1909 telephoto. The Trango Towers were profiled through Conway Saddle on the last morning of our traverse. Then came the Gasherbrums, I, II, III, and IV, filling the western sky. We had hoped for a view of K2 or Broad Peak, but they remained hidden behind the greatest row of lesser peaks on earth (all four Gasherbrums being among the seventeen highest mountains).

Ski mountaineers traversing face of Mt. Sia Kangri at 22,500 feet.

The last day to Conway Saddle was a seemingly endless traverse through seracs and cliffs. Just before sunset only one final barrier separated us from the rim of the Baltoro basin (and imagined security for the remainder of our journey). A short overhang dropped onto a steep snow slope that soon plunged into the mile-deep chasm. I was lowered—pack, skis, and all—from two ice screws. The sled tugged at my waist, and I spent long minutes thrashing my way on my knees to a spot where I could stomp out a platform. Dan followed in nearly as awkward fashion. Kim and Ned planned to lower their packs and sleds, then climb down. It was a great plan, but almost a tragic end to the trip. Ned's pack with all his personal survival gear and a stove came unclipped from the rope. I ran for it, stumbled, and missed. Below me, the pack began a straight shot for the Kondus, interrupted at the last moment by Dan's flying tackle. He made a tremendous end run across the slope and, without a moment's hesitation, jumped on the seventy-pound bundle armored with crampons like a lineman for the Steelers.

The next day we made a steep but straightforward descent to the Abruzzi Glacier. Dan and Ned turned around to see yet another wild bundle hurtling out of control. Kim's sled shot by at tremendous speed, followed immediately by roaring laughter. Kim, tired of being passed by his sled and tripped by its cords, had purposely let it fly into a smooth basin where it came to a gradual stop. That night we camped opposite the icefall of the South Gasherbrum Glacier, a place made forever mystical by the poetic musings of Fosco Maraini in his classic book, *Karakoram: The Ascent of Gasherbrum IV*.

Karakoram pundits had warned us that the upper Baltoro and Abruzzi glaciers were riddled with huge crevasses, making travel difficult, circuitous, and dangerous. Early in the year we found precisely the opposite conditions. A veritable highway about two hundred feet wide followed the arcs of the moraines as far as we could see. On either side of this perfect ski path was jumbled ice and rock. After double-poling gently mile after mile, we touched our first rock and drank our first running water in eleven days.

The weather had been good to us. After a few

mild storms on the Siachen we enjoyed a week of mostly clear skies for our high traverse. As we headed down the Baltoro, skies blackened and temperatures soared far higher than they should have for the loss of elevation. We had experienced five straight nights below $-20°$ F, and now we began a longer string of nights over twenty above, a phenomenal shift of forty degrees. Heat, not cold, became our greatest adversary. By nine each morning the hard snow was collapsing under our skis, and with loads still over a hundred pounds, we sank into baseless depth hoar of the worst order.

On the morning of April 18th I awoke just a few miles above Concordia, where the Baltoro and Godwin-Austen glaciers join in a great amphitheater in full view of K2. The clouds were lowering quickly, and I asked the others' permission to pack up and leave early. By five a.m. I was gliding easily on the hard surface, remembering a day five years before when I had also been alone on the moraines of Concordia. In 1975 after an attempt on K2 a mail runner had handed me a bulky envelope from my mother in California. It contained my 90-year-old father's ashes. He had died while I was on the mountain, and I left the group that day to release his remains to the winds over a moraine of pure marble. The letter from my mother had compared the tranquility of his face in death to a fine marble bust, and I felt fortunate to find the same material in its raw state.

The 1980 morning was bleak and gray. My spirits were low until I rounded a corner and saw K2 for the first time on this trip, rising over a great block of white marble. Tears ran down my cheeks, and I sat down to absorb the simultaneous emotions triggered by memories of my father and the mountain. For an hour the mountain showed its top above the clouds. Just before the others arrived, it disappeared, never to be seen for the remainder of our journey.

Below Concordia our natural path ended. Rivers of melt water sealed us off from the most inviting corridors of travel. The landscape looked as if God's own construction company had torn it up and left it unfinished. Moraines marched infinitely in every direction, presenting jagged rocks toward the sun and a marginal snow layer in the shade. It was a skier's Hell.

Day after day we got up at 3:30 a.m., thrashed partly on skis, partly on foot with giant loads, ate from our fast-eroding supplies, and slowed from a peak speed of four miles an hour on the Upper Baltoro to an agonizing four miles a day.

One morning, after eating a gourmet breakfast of soup concocted from the last spoonfuls of instant potatoes, I moaned to Kim, "How are we going to get through this?" He turned to me with a confident air, and said, "I think I have the answer."

Kim was our medical officer. Although not a doctor, he had a strongly developed historical sense of medication for mountaineering. He knew of a drug that had been developed precisely for this purpose by native people who found it necessary to carry tremendous loads at high elevations with low caloric intakes. Small amounts of this extract from a South American leaf were at one time a main ingredient in the most successful multinational soft drink until the potential for abuse made it illegal. Propitiously, Kim had been able to purchase an ounce of this material at the Khyber Pass to add to our medical kit.

Kim and I were tentmates and we decided that our medical experiment needed a valid control group. Ned and Dan, unlike us, were not complainers. They were members of the stiff-upper-lip school who never swore when their sleds passed them, nor beat their sleds into submission when they attacked one's feet or became tangled in one's skis. We had been moving at relatively equal rates, and we thought it fitting that the non-complainers should continue unaware.

At noon that day we waited an hour and a half for them. In the evening we waited yet another hour. Sleep, of course, also had to be induced by drugs, but the entire process was repeated successfully day after day until we arrived in Askole about twenty-five pounds lighter than when we began.

After three days of gorging and resting, we set out on the last leg of our journey. Dan decided to stay behind, partly because of sore knees and partly from a desire to help the efficiency of our travel. Three of us could cut our weight by using one tent, one rope, and one stove. Without the climbing gear or extreme clothing needed for the first leg, we were able to start with a more reasonable 95 pounds each.

We hired nine Askole porters to carry for three days until we could ski on the Biafo Glacier. Our sirdar was Hadji Ali, who had carried my father's ashes up the Baltoro as a mail runner in 1975. He was an old hunter with a keen eye for wildlife, and we were amazed at the profuse evidence of large mammals living above the inhabited valleys. On my first trip to the Karakoram, George Schaller and I had found the Baltoro region sadly depleted of wildlife. Inexplicably, the Biafo was another story. Nearly every side canyon beyond Mango Brangsa at 12,200 feet had ibex tracks in the snow. I counted more than fifty animals in one day. A major recession of the ice had left level, moist moats on either side of the glacier, and these were pocked with the footprints of brown bear, snow leopard, fox, and ibex. Farther up the glacier a lammergeier landed within 200 feet of us, only to soar with its nine-foot wing spread toward the granite faces bordering the glacier.

Here, lining the sides of the upper Biafo, was the greatest display of granite spires in the entire Karakoram, marching up the glacier like organ pipes in an ordered procession. Enough major climbs to last several generations were spread around us, untouched and unnamed. The Bilafond and Saltoro valleys also had considerably more large granite faces than the fabled Baltoro, but for aesthetics the Biafo won, hands down.

An icefall at the top of the Hispar La was a nonevent, buried so completely in snow that we encountered no crevasse problems. A snowstorm forced us to camp directly on top of the 16,900-foot pass, and when it cleared we were treated to a superb view of the Ogre rising above a cloud bank in the moonlight. The fresh snow gave us sixteen miles of downhill powder skiing the next day. Too soon we were back on mixed ground again as the snow cover gradually ran out. Just eight and a half days after leaving Askole, we walked into the village of Hispar. Two more days of hiking and a short jeep ride brought us to Hunza and the end of our journey.

It would be nice to conclude with an image of ski-mountaineers gamboling through the green fields of fabled Hunza, overcome with the sensual flow of returning to the living world. To do so would intimate that we found the dream of the campfires of my youth. What we found at the end of six weeks of the most intense physical activity of our lives was sensory and social deprivation. At our first dinner in a hotel, I said, not really believing it myself, "Isn't it wonderful to return to hot water and cold beer?"

Kim held a thousand-yard stare and answered, "The special things I miss are not what we're finding here, but what we've left behind in the dusty villages and campsites in the snow." Somehow, we had lost much of our capacity to enjoy not only the wonderful excesses of civilized life, but also the clean, simple emotions of love and beauty that color all heights of experience. Never on a mere peak-climbing expedition had any of us undergone such a shift. Among us were those who found the mountains of the Karakoram undistinguished and our partners little more worthy of intimacy than passengers on an elevator. I believe that we experienced to a lesser degree the same sort of mental and physical trauma that left most survivors of Auschwitz unable to laugh or love for a long time. Dan summed up all our immediate feelings when he told a newspaper reporter, "The trip was hardly enjoyable; it was an accomplishment."

Today, almost three years after the expedition, I still feel its effects. I no longer dream of that ideal expedition, "isolated from the rest of humanity and any need to depend upon it." I know the reality, the trade-offs, and the strange mental filtration that has turned it into the favorite mountain adventure of my life.

18
Cholatse:
The Last
Virgin of
the Khumbu

IN APRIL 1982, while the first Russian expedition was climbing Mount Everest from Nepal with a cast of nearly a thousand climbers and porters, five of us attempted Cholatse, the last named, unclimbed peak in the Everest region. We felt almost smugly certain of success. Our team was strong and our motives were fitting and proper. We had avoided pre-climb publicity, funded cash costs entirely out of members' pockets, planned not to use porters above base camp, and brought the latest equipment, courtesy of several manufacturers. The mountain—however hard it might prove to be—was only 21,130 feet. Furthermore, all five members had previously seen Cholatse and believed it could be rushed up and down in two to three days with good weather.

We were unanimous in underestimating the mountain. The white coating that appeared to be snow on our chosen southwest arête turned out to be brittle ice for thousands of feet. To complicate matters, unseasonal pre-monsoon storms brought wind and snow every afternoon.

Opposite page: Cholatse from the west. Ascent followed ridge just in from right skyline.

187

Before the climb I led a two-week photography trek in the same region, passing countless yak caravans loaded with bright-colored duffles, trekkers in even more vivid hues, and Sherpas decked out in boots, jackets, and specialty items that were only just hitting stores in the United States. It was hard to keep in mind that just thirty-two years earlier no westerner had ever visited the Khumbu homeland of the Sherpas. In that short span, the Khumbu had become the Mecca of the Himalayas, visited by far more people than any other region so close to a great peak. More than 8,000 trekkers and climbers from around the world came in 1982, mostly bound for Everest Base Camp. The finely shaped lower peaks—Ama Dablam, Thamserku, Kantega—were climbed legally or illegally by the middle 1960s. Why Cholatse had gone untouched was something of a mystery. It was a bit too hard to climb illegally without attracting attention, but no one knew for certain why it had been kept off the permitted list.

Cholatse, sometimes spelled Tsolatse or given the Tibetan name, Jobo Lhaptshan, became the "last virgin of the Khumbu" not by way of virtue, but by paternal restrictions begun by the Ministry of Tourism when the mountains of Nepal first opened in 1950. Cholatse's continued closure was more a quirk of bureaucracy than the result of a clear rationale. It was not worth a large peak fee, and it was hidden up the Gokyo Valley, lacking the obvious appeal of mountains closer to the classic route to Everest Base Camp. Another consideration was that some Sherpas considered Cholatse a very sacred mountain, one of five goddesses surrounding Everest. Others said the peak had no special significance. The head lama of the famous Thyangboche Monastery told me simply, "All mountains are sacred."

Four years earlier, Al Read, director of Mountain Travel Nepal, had asked me to join a prospective Cholatse climb. He kept after the government until they finally gave him a permit late in 1981. As late as six weeks before departure, the expedition had no funding, no equipment, and just two certain climbers:

Peter Hackett and myself. Read had a busy trekking season, and he decided to "godfather" the expedition rather than actively climb himself. He had also invited Bill O'Connor, a British mountaineer with considerable Himalayan experience. Peter and I decided on a minimum of four climbers for an alpine-style attempt on what appeared to be a safe but steep ridge. We invited Vern Clevenger and John Roskelley to round out the team.

We met in Kathmandu and sent our gear ahead with porters, saving some of the cost of flying it to the high airstrip at Lukla. The others took off on a two-week acclimatizing trek while I was with my photography group. On the morning of April 15th I left them in a village not far from Lukla and took off toward Cholatse with one strong porter. We covered five normal trekking days in one, reaching a point half an hour below our base camp at dusk in clouds so thick that we couldn't find our way up the remaining trail-less hill. The next morning I arrived to spot the other four heading out of base camp for the peak. I stayed back to rest while they spent the day establishing a route through a long icefall to a col at 18,600 feet where an advanced camp could be placed. A fixed line was placed on the final six-hundred-foot headwall to help haul loads on the final push. They returned to base camp late in the day.

For the next four days it stormed; not all the time but just enough to quell our enthusiasm. The morning of April 20th was clear. We regained the col with food for two more days, and fixed three ropes on the hard ice above. In the afternoon it snowed yet again.

The next morning was clear, but Hackett was too sick to climb. A world expert in mountain medicine, he was quite sure that his ailment was short-lived and not due to altitude. We faced a triangle of awful decisions: wait a day or two and not have enough food to attempt the climb; leave a sick man alone, a man whose desire for Cholatse and whose efforts on behalf of the expedition exceeded any of our own; or make multiple trips through the icefall, which, due to hanging glaciers above, Hackett felt was as dangerous as

the Khumbu Icefall on Everest. We trusted his judg-
ment. Just six months before he had gone through
that icefall on his way to the top of Everest.

After considerable discussion Hackett volunteered to stay at the col camp until we returned from
the attempt. To fail on a lower peak after so recent a
success on Everest was hard to swallow. He said goodbye, then crawled into his bag as we jumared slowly up
the ropes above the col.

Hackett's wasn't the only failure. On previous
light expeditions where we had brought our own
timeworn gear, I had rarely witnessed an equipment
failure. That day Vern's crampons sheared a front
screw. A new superwide strap tore off my crampon at
the rivet. John's "Lifetime" ice tool broke off clean at
the adze. By noon my digital watch was in pieces, and
I had hacked big chunks of foam out of the new Al-
veolite inners of my plastic boots to try to make them
fit something larger than a ballet dancer's heel. To
top things off we came to the only feasible campsite
far too early in the day. At just 19,000 feet it seemed
much too low for a round trip to the top the next day.

In the afternoon Clevenger and O'Connor cut a
tent platform out of hard ice while Roskelley and I
fixed our four climbing ropes on the steep ridge
above. On the last lead I stopped to place two ice
screws for protection across a traverse of an 80°
bulge. After Roskelley followed, he said, "Any one of
us can climb anything on this mountain, but we're going to have to get up this fast, or we're not going to
make it. I'm the fastest, and I can lead most of this
without protection if it's okay with everybody."

It was. One day's food remained after two days of
climbing. We were up at 3:30 a.m., the tents were left
in place, and Roskelley led off. Pitch after pitch of
steep ice went by without the placing of a single point
of protection. "Ready?" Roskelley would say with two
ice tools stuck in the wall. I would pay out rope continuously for ten minutes as he climbed with thirty
pounds on his back until the rope ran out. Then he
would place ice screws for a belay, and I would follow.
Clevenger and O'Connor would follow later, pulling

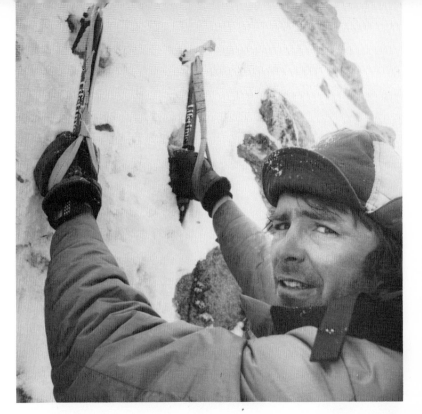

out the ropes and screws for use above.

John Roskelley on the southwest ridge of Cholatse.

Fifteen rope lengths of steep ice—2,250 feet—brought us to the summit plateau by noon. We cached some gear and headed on with O'Connor in the lead. When a massive crevasse blocked the route, Roskelley did an end run up yet another ice pitch. There we found not the summit, but a hidden three-hundred-foot ice headwall. After twelve long hours of climbing, Roskelley and Clevenger reached the top in a full blizzard with their hair on end from electricity in the air. O'Connor and I joined them minutes later, and we all beat a hasty retreat.

It was too late to attempt a descent to the high camp, so we stomped out a platform at the top of the ridge and camped without a tent or bivvy sacks in a mild snowstorm. Lightning flashed in the southern sky over India as we heated water for one freeze-dried dinner between us. The others were testing Quallofil bags that would hold their loft when wet. Mine had torn a seam before the climb, so I had brought a

down bag instead. Knowing that it would collapse like a wet sock as soon as my body heat melted the falling snow, I wore boots, overboots, and a one-piece climbing suit to bed.

In the morning the temperature was −2° F., my bag felt like a giant Pepsi bottle, but I was warm inside my waterproof garments, as were the others in their fluffy bags. As the first light hit Makalu, Everest, and Ama Dablam, we packed up to begin twenty frightening diagonal rappels back down the ridge, which overhung to the south most of the way down. Our loads grew lighter as we consumed almost all of our ice hardware for anchors every 150 feet.

At the col Peter greeted us, recovered from a short bout with the flu, but still a bit weak. He joined us, and we continued our descent toward base camp. Just below the glacier we were met by a welcoming committee that included Al Read, his family, several friends, and our Sherpas. A "Welcome Home Cholatse Expedition" sign graced an arch of willow branches over a gate in the stone yak corral at the entrance to camp. The Sherpas were preparing a victory dinner and baking a cake for us.

A more idyllic return from a climb is hard to imagine. We were far off any trekking route, camped in a meadow eye-to-eye with peaks on the other side of the Gokyo Valley, sharing our joy with a few friends.

The next morning I walked over the hill to watch the clouds. Below me two figures were sitting by a rock—our Sherpas watching the same movements of land and sky. On the next hill three local herdsmen also sat looking. Each group was separate, yet motivated by similar emotions. None of us would have come here and shared this experience without our particular ulterior motives. Our Sherpas were hired hands on an expedition, the herdsmen were tending their family yaks, and our objective was to climb a mountain. Trekkers on a trail might have snapped a picture or two, but invariably they would have kept on walking instead of sitting down to silently soak in the world around them.

I saw how little the essential values of the

Opposite page:
Ice climbing on
Cholatse.

Khumbu have changed with the recent onslaught of
tourists. We were able to share the essence of these
mountains with those who lived in them, just as the
first Khumbu travelers had done thirty years before.

One of the reasons Sherpas integrate so well with
westerners is that unlike hill farmers or merchants,
they have no single life purpose. They herd, they
farm, they trade, they work for trekkers and climbers.

A typical Sherpa family lives on an acre of land in
a town within sight of the mountains. Their children
walk to school with no fear of trouble on the way or in
class. They raise their own livestock, grow their own
vegetables. For part of the year the husband travels,
making a better salary than in town. He brings things
back from exotic places and tells exciting stories
around the fireplace. While he was gone his wife managed the land, the animals, and represented the family in frequent community affairs. Together they travel to other villages and visit their summer home in a
high meadow.

An hour below our Cholatse base camp was a
cluster of fields and stone buildings that comprise the
summer settlement of Na. Called *yersas*, these Sherpa
summer homes are set in high-altitude pastures where
yaks and goats graze during the warmest parts of the
year. In one building I had tea with Sonam Dorje,
eighteen-year-old son of a Sherpa from Phortse who
has been on eleven Everest expeditions. All the Na
yersas were owned by Phortse families. Sonam had
worked on several commercial treks, but he told me
he would not be doing such work for two more years.
"I'll be staying here from March to August. Sometimes my father comes; sometimes I'm alone. When
one of my four brothers is old enough to stay here,
I'll go back to work as a trekking Sherpa."

With his previous earnings from trekking he
could have easily bought a transistor radio, like many
of the lowland Nepalese who now violate the quiet air
of their villages. Instead, Sonam bought a pressure
cooker to save precious fuel for cooking potatoes and
vegetables at his 14,500-foot summer home. On the
wall he had hung art paper with Tibetan characters

which he learned to draw at school. Next to his work hung a Marlboro ad and a *Time* cover.

The juxtaposition was not as disturbing as it seems. On another family's wall I spotted a picture from *Time* of the musician, Rostropovich, and his wife. I learned that the family had put it up simply because it captured an expression of love between husband and wife. They had no idea who the people were.

After a rest day, several of us decided to extend our trek home by crossing the Cho La, a 17,800-foot pass connecting the Gokyo Valley with Pheriche on the Everest trekking route. Our intent was simply to see more of the region around the peak we had climbed, but in another sense our urge to circle around a mountain meaningful to us was exactly what reverent Tibetan Buddhists do with landmarks that have special meanings in their lives.

How different our Khumbu experience was from that of the Russians on Everest. Their memories would be weighted toward months in a sterile world, while only four days of our month were actually on the heights. Those four intense days, however, had paid us wonderful dividends for an extremely low investment. By cutting corners in every way, our month's lightweight expedition and trek with a Sherpa crew and government-required liaison officer (kept warm and content in a nearby Namche Bazar guesthouse at our expense) ended up costing less than half the tarriff of most commercial Khumbu treks. The entire expedition except for Peter reached the summit of an unclimbed peak, and more importantly, returned healthy and happy—the true bottom line of a successful expedition.

High
and Wild

"I welcome wholeheartedly the
advance of modern techniques
because it has widened the
bounds or mountain adventure.
There was a time, long ago, when
I was oppressed by the thought
that soon there would be no
peaks to climb and no new routes
to explore. But the more I
travelled in the remoter
ranges . . . the more I realized
how vast is the field of fresh
endeavor. . . . With the
application of these new climbing
and survival techniques, the
horizon is truly boundless."

Eric Shipton
That Untravelled World

Glossary

Aid: artificial climbing in which mechanical aids such as **pitons, bolts,** and ropes are used for body support. The same equipment may be used for **free climbing,** but for safety only, not as a means of upward climbing or resting.

Aid slings: stirrups usually made from inch-wide nylon tape. They are used as rope ladders and attached to anchors by **carabiners.**

Alpine style: an increasingly popular method of climbing even major peaks in which the climbers ascend as a self-contained unit without relying on porters or previously provisioned camps.

Angle piton: a piton made for cracks half-inch wide and larger. A cross section resembles the long sides of the letter "A".

Arête: a steep and narrow ridge on a mountain or rock wall.

Bat hook: a device used for **direct aid** in shallow drilled holes, invented by Warren Harding to save time on long blank cliffs where **bolts** would otherwise be necessary.

Belay: as a verb this word means to feed rope to the

leader from a secure position so that the climber can be held in case of a fall. As a noun **belay** means the entire safety system on which the leader depends.

Bergschrund: a crevasse, usually large, at the edge of a glacier separating a mountain and a glacier.

Bivouac: in climbing, a night spent during the course of a climb without full gear such as tents.

Bolt: see **expansion bolt**

Buttress: an outside corner or projection of a mountain or cliff somewhat wider than an **arête.**

Cairn: a pile of rocks left as a marker on a summit or as a means of indicating a route, similar to a blaze on a tree.

Carabiner: a metal snap-link about three inches long which resembles a giant safety pin and is capable of holding more than a ton. Carabiners are used for attaching the rope to anchors in rock or snow.

Chimney: a long crack large enough for a person to enter, often climbed by cross-pressure between knees, back, feet and hands. When a chimney is narrow it is called a squeeze chimney, and if it is narrower yet, a **jam crack.**

Chocks: see **nuts**

Class one, two, three, four, five, and six: parts of a rating system for the difficulty of climbs. **Classes one through four** do not require belaying through anchors. **Class five** is **free climbing** using a **belay** and **pitons, nuts, runners,** or **bolts** for protection. **Class six** is aid climbing. The difficulty of free climbing is expressed in decimals of **class five,** 5.1 being easy and 5.9 being very difficult. As standards have progressed, climbers have found it necessary to add 5.10 to 5.12, but **class six** is rated by the symbols A1 to A5. Not only are fewer categories need for **aid** climbing, but to use decimals of the number six would be confusing since **class five** climbs are often more difficult than **class six.**

Col: a high pass, usually between two peaks; from the French word for shoulder.

Couloir: from the French word for hallway, a gully in the side of a mountain.

Crampons: metal spikes attached to climbing boots; essential for climbing ice or hard snow.

Dihedral: an inside corner where two rock planes intersect. Sometimes called an **open book** because of the resemblance to a partly oened book. Cracks usually occur at the intersection, and dihedrals are an important part of route-finding, especially on **granite faces**.

Direct aid: see **aid** and **class six**

Expansion bolt: a device designed for anchoring in concrete which climbers use in drilled hole when cracks are not available for **pitons** or **nuts**.

Face climbing: utilizing foot and hand holds on an open rock face as opposed to **jamming, chimneying,** or using **aid**.

Fixed rope: a rope left in place after a pitch is climbed so that climbers can ascend or descend at will. To **fix** a pitch means to climb a distance and leave a rope.

Free climbing: climbing in which upward progress is entirely unsupported by mechanial aids. A rope and hardware may be used for safety only. The opposite of **aid**, artifical climbing. (See **class five**)

Friction or **friction climbing: face climbing** on **slabs** where foot and handholds are slanted and the climber uses friction rather than defined holds.

Front pointing: using only the front points of **crampons** to ascend steep ice or snow.

Jam crack: a crack running vertically which is climbed by jamming part of the body into the fissure. A thin jam crack may be only large enough for a climber's fingers, whereas a wide jam may admit a shoulder and a leg. A jam crack large enough to admit the climber's whole body is called a **chimney.**

Jumars: mechanical ascenders used to climb **fixed ropes** and often to follow behind the leader on long climbs. Jumars grip the rope when pulled down, but slide freely upward so that with a foot slings a climber can ascend a 150-foot rope in a matter of minutes. (See **Prusik**)

Lieback (sometimes written as **layback**): crack climbing using counterpressure between hands and feet.

Nuts: artificial chockstones usually made of aluminum alloy and threaded with nylon cord. They are fitted into constrictions in cracks, and can be used most of the time in place of **pitons,** which scar the rock if removed and replaced frequently.

Pitch: a unit measure of climbing, meaning a distance covered in one rope length. Some pitches may be nearly as lng as the rope (150-165 feet). Others may be as short as 50 feet if they are difficult and there is no stopping place above.

Pitons: a metal wedge driven into a natural crack in the rock with a hole or a ring at one end for attching a carabiner. Pitons come in all sizes from Rurps, which are the size of postage stamps that fit fingernail-thick cracks to bong-bongs, which fit cracks wider than a man's foot.

Prusik: a technique for climbing a rope. This word was originally confined to the use of Prusik knots but is now used for rope climbing with **jumar** ascenders. The knot, invented by Karl Prusik many years ago, will slide freely when unweighted but grips tightly to the main rope when weight is applied to it.

Rappel: a technique for descending a rope in which friction of the rope across the body or through **carabiners** is used to control the rate of descent. A doubled rope is used so that it can be retrieved by pulling one end, requiring only the leaving of **piton** or sling anchors at wide distances on the descent of a climb.

Rope traverse: see **tension traverse**

Runners: loops of nylon rope or tape that have many purposes. They can be used in place of **pitons** or **nuts** to make the rope run more easily; they are like baling wire to the mechanic—often used to temporarily attach almost anything to anything else.

Scree: a collection of small, loose rocks, usually below a cliff. **Talus** is collection of larger loose rocks that normally don't slide when you walk on them.

Skyhook: a small hook used for **aid** on tiny ledges when cracks are not available for **nuts** or **pitons.**

Slab: a smooth section of a cliff which is steep but

somewhat less than vertical.

Tension traverse: direct-aid climbing in which a climber crosses a traverse with the aid of a tight rope from behind, using hands and feet on the rock to counterbalance the side pull of the rope.

A Note
on the
Photography

THE FIRST EDITION of *High and Wild* was a four-color production that showed wilderness scenes in colors as real as color photography and printing could make them. For this paperback edition, black-and-white conversions were made from the original color transparencies by means of low-contrast 4 × 5 internegatives. Only those transparencies that converted well into black-and-white were selected. A very few images were originally shot with balck-and-white film.

To record the spontaneity of high and wild experiences, I use only 35mm equipment. Taking large-format cameras into the wilderness is too much of a compromise with adventure for me. While I admire the clarity of images made with such cameras, their usefulness in photographing wilderness adventures is limited by their cumbersomeness, which makes it nearly impossible to capture a companion in the act of skiing or climbing. Without incredibly heavy lenses, they cannot photograph distant wildlife or scenes. For still scenes, I handle the 35mm camera as if it were a 4 × 5. Instead of taking a quick, handheld shot, I use a tripod and slow, fine-grained film; and I spend lots of time composing and selecting the right aperture for my desired zone of focus. Yet the same equipment gives me the freedom to record action as it occures. My basic equipment for going light is a Nikon FM2 with 24mm and 85mm lenses. Depending on the need, I also bring along one or more of the following: 20mm, 35mm, 45mm, 55mm, 75-150mm zoom, 200mm, 400mm, 500mm, and 600mm lenses, as well as macro and perspective-control lenses. I also carry a second camera, a fully automatic f3 with a motordrive.

I keep the first camera loaded with Kodachrome 25, the best transparency film for sharpness and latitude (the range of detail a film picks up in shadows and highlights). Its colors are less harsh than its cousin, Kodachrome 64, which I use in the second camera when extra film speed is need for action, wildlife, or night photography.

Kodachrome 25 has almost zero response to ultraviolet light, which can make Kodachrome 64 go blue at higher altitude unless a UV filter is used on every lens. I seldom use films faster than ASA 64 because, unless the light is very even, films over ASA 100 tend to produce harsh-looking slides that end up in my wastebasket. I do not use "fish-eyes" or extreme telephotos because I wish to record what I see, not an image obviously altered by equipment. I do not use filters to alter the tone of an entire scene, other than a very mild Nikon A2 that removes the bluish tint from shadows. A polarizer was used for about ten percent of these photgraphs.

When taking photographs, I am always aware of how each natural color will appear on film. Only by consciously thinking about the limitations of the film can I visualize how the image will appear. Tones of red, for instance, vary greatly in different exposures of the same scene. True blacks are rarely seen by the eye; nearly every black silhouette in this book was actually illuminated with enough light to read by. Many beautiful sights are impossible to transfer onto film; rather than intrude my camera into an experience for no purpose, I simply enjoy them.

Wilderness photographs are like gems: the real and the synthetic are often indistinguishable. The photos in this book have for me, a stamp of reality that I find missing in images I sometimes "create" on editorial or advertising assignments: nearly all of my favorite photographs are ones that I was not seeking in the first place. The unexpected in nature always provides the greatest artistic opportunity, and capturing such a moment is rarely just the result of being in the right place at the right time. It is a blend of intuitive thinking and technical discipline, a coming together of the two halves of the brain to see with an artist's eye while operating equipment precisely.